PRISMS

FOR A CHRIST-LIFE

About the icon
  Christ the Holy Silence

This rendition of an eighteenth-century Russian icon calling us into silence is naturally difficult to put into words. The enigmatic aura of this icon, which grows with silent conversation, greatly contributes to its drawing power. Holy Silence is an allegorical representation both of Christ as the feminine Sophia and of the Silence of the Suffering Servant of Isaiah's prophecy, and it is also a vision or reminder of the mystical Russian Jesus prayer. The earliest known image of Holy Wisdom as feminine comes from a manuscript of the fourteenth century from Mt. Sinai.

—William Hart McNichols SJ

PRISMS

FOR A CHRIST-LIFE

David L. Fleming SJ

Review for Religious
St. Louis, Missouri 63108

Acknowledgment

The publisher gratefully acknowleges the use on the cover—
by permission of the artist—of the icon Christ the Holy Silence.

The publisher also acknowledges the permission to use the English
translation of psalms, antiphons, and scripture readings from
The Liturgical Psalter©1995, International Committee on English in
the Liturgy, Inc. All rights reserved.

Scripture translations on page 38 and pages 70-71 are from the text
of *The New American Bible*©1970 by the Confraternity of Christian
Doctrine, Washington, D.C.

Review for Religious
3601 Lindell Boulevard
St. Louis, Missouri 63108

ISBN 0-924768-10-X

contents

introduction

looking at evangelization

looking for Jesus Christ

looking for the spirit

looking for the father

looking at the church year

looking for a spiritual life

looking at religious life

Looking in a Different Way

Prisms can be understood as perspectives that allow us to see things in different or varying ways. To be able to view our world, its peoples, and its various situations through different crystal-configurations can be likened to entering into God's expansive vision in our own small and faltering way. We Christians are truly blessed in having Jesus as a prism for our privileged understanding of God and God's dealings with our world.

We find our human formation and education introduced through various prisms. Literature and art throughout the ages have given us a way of seeing nature and our own humanity through eyes not our own. The breakthroughs of science and technology happen because people take a new look at a given reality and see a previously unnoticed set of relationships or pierce through a complexity to a simplifying of its elements. All of these human ways of sharing insight into the makeup and relationship of our everyday world are part of what I want to include in my use of the word *prisms*.

Without *prisms* we languish in a kind of *prison* (to play upon a "sound-alike" word), the prison of our own myopic vision. Prisms are important for the healthiness of our spiritual, moral, and intellectual life. Unless we are able to break out of our own limited way of knowing, we are caught in the prison of our limited experience, of our particular culture, and of our own historical period. We need an openness to looking at our life and our world with new eyes our whole life long. This is what it means "to really live," "to be alive."

The great gift of our Catholic faith includes its own special gift of prisms for us. Our faith, because it is truly catholic, gives us new ways of seeing ourselves, God, our neighbor, and our world. Faith is not a single, once-for-all-time vision, but ways of seeing that continue to open upon new vistas in every time and culture. Personally, too, our faith continues to expand our vision and stimulates us to keep growing. Of course, for such a continuing growth to happen, we need to cooperate with God's grace by our praying, by our reading of the Gospel, by listening to the word of God broken open in homilies, by reflecting upon the conversations and life-situations that are a daily part of life.

Some ten years ago, as editor of Review for Religious, I began to write an introductory reflection called Prisms in each issue of the journal. Many people have encouraged me to collect and publish these reflections in a more permanent way. I have edited, revised, and sometimes expanded a number of those reflections, and they now form the content of this book. It is my hope that in their brief form they may stimulate your personal reflections on your own faith living and so further your spiritual growth. It is also my hope that these prisms might be an occasion for deepening your prayer about some basic issues of Christian life. To help in this movement to prayer, I have concluded each reflection with a psalm selection or a scripture passage that complements the hue and value of the reflection.

I express my gratitude to Father William Hart McNichols SJ for his permission to have his icon rendition of *Christ the Holy Silence* grace the cover of this book. I need not belabor the fact that icons truly are prisms into the holy, and this particular icon is most appropriate for the theme of this book. I am also indebted to John R. Page, executive secretary for the International Commission on English in the Liturgy, for the express permission to reproduce the ICEL translation of *The Liturgical Psalter* (1995) for psalms and scripture readings used in the prayer reflections. Two scripture readings (p. 38 and pp. 70-71) are from the text of *The New American Bible* (1970) by the

Confraternity of Christian Doctrine, Washington, D.C.

Finally, I thank the staff of Review for Religious, particularly Father Philip C. Fischer SJ, Mary Ann Foppe, and Tracy Gramm for their invaluable help in seeing this book through to its final production.

We can be grateful that our Catholic faith provides us with many prisms, many bright facets and lusters. But our living of our faith will be as rich as the sustained use we make of its many prisms—always (re)viewing life in our time and in our culture through the eyes of Jesus Christ.

David L. Fleming SJ

The Call to a New Evangelization

History happens. We human beings can write our history books and, by emphasis and omission and sometimes by romanticizing, make as if we are masters of our history. It may take only some seventy years for the rewriting of the Communist history of Russia or it may take five hundred years for the European discovery of the Americas to be reevaluated. But it happens.

We say that Pope John XXIII made history when he called the Second Vatican Council. We are well aware that the church experienced, through the actions of the bishops present at the council, something that has been likened to a second Pentecost. For our own availability to the God of history, we need to return again and again to the happening of that first Pentecost and the subsequent events as recorded in the Acts of the Apostles. God's Spirit makes things happen, even when the very persons involved seem so little capable of being the crafters of history. Most recently Pope John Paul II has expressed his own desire to make history by his call for a new evangelization, particularly occasioned by our entering into the third millennium. This call to a new evangelization holds the promise of another moment of this second Pentecost that came with Vatican II. It is history hap-

13

pening, in which none of us is the master or control-artist, but every one of us plays an important role—with the Spirit's direction.

Evangelization—new evangelization—demands much of us all. A paradigm of evangelization and inculturation captures our attention anew as we reflect upon the events in the Acts of the Apostles. It means that no one can hold himself or herself exempt from the call of this second moment of the second Pentecost—the call to a new hearing of good news. This is not the time for new rules or the imposition of old ones—the Judaizers tried that two thousand years ago. It is the time for Cornelius, his wife, and household to invite Peter once again to proclaim the gospel so that new conversion on everyone's part can take place. It is the time for Peter to dream new dreams and hear God telling him that old restrictions do not apply in a new creation moment.

One of the deepest meanings of Pentecost lies in the fact that all peoples heard the good news in a way that they could understand and respond to. It goes beyond the language barrier to breakthroughs involving customs, heritages, and rituals. In the Pentecost beginnings, Jesus Christ and the gospel message needed no inculturation. In the new evangelization as in the original one recorded in the Acts of the Apostles, it is not Jesus Christ who needs to be inculturated; he is already a confidant of people's hearts. It is his church that must be inculturated by being evangelized anew as well as by evangelizing others. The Acts of the Apostles—the story of the first evangelizing time—portrays the exhilarating and somber picture that inculturating a church does not come without cost—a cost which everyone must bear in listening to shocking good news, in experiencing a certain amount of turmoil, in suffering the pain of differences expressed vigorously by people who serve or are served.

John Paul II has said that "we need an evangelization that is new in its ardor, new in its method, new in its expressions." That is what we—always the disciples—must allow to happen to ourselves first: to be evangelized anew in order to be the new evangelizers. We need to rethink how to inculturate a church, not a gospel. If the original Jewish and pagan converts to the new Christian faith seemed to share little common religious heritage and ritual and yet, with struggle, came to form the

Body of Christ, can we today not recognize the imperative of a new evangelization demanding the same kind of breakthrough for traditionalists, liberals, feminists, or whatever modern-day version an appeal to the party of Apollos or Paul takes?

A new evangelization brings the excitement of discovery into our own lives and so into our church. Let the Spirit lead. It has happened; it will happen again.

Let Us Pray

**I join heaven's chorus,
praising your love and fidelity.**

*I thank you with all I am,
I join heaven's chorus.
I bow toward your holy temple,
to praise your name.*

*By your love and fidelity,
you display to all
the glory of your name and promise.
As soon as I call, you act,
renewing my strength.*

*Around the world,
rulers praise you
for your commanding word.
They sing of your ways,
"Great is your glory, Lord."*

PSALM 138:1-5

The Attitude for Evangelization

For most people there is a healthy anticipation of "good things" when new beginnings are made. Perhaps such "anticipation" should be called, rather, a precious grace which interconnects us with God, the eternal optimist.

New evangelization is the most consistently optimistic theme of John Paul II's papacy. While his encyclicals and apostolic exhortations are many and weighty, I suspect that his repeated call to a new evangelization will be the most significant and lasting grace for the church. The call is a beginning similar to the beginning of a year; it is not as if evangelization is any newer than the parade of days which form any year's calendar. The newness in large part comes from the attitude with which we enter into evangelization, just as it comes from the way we enter into another year.

The oft-quoted phrase about this call to evangelization being "new in its vigor, new in its methods, and new in its expression" is grounded in the *attitude* which we bring to our Christian responsibility as evangelizers. Attitude alone is not enough, but unless the grace of optimism warms our efforts as believers in Good News to share it and explain it and to offer people a challenge, little evangelization is the result.

For example, we sometimes consider women and men religious as primary evangelizers, giving example for all of us in the church. Do members of religious congregations need to see a more intimate connection between the new evangelization and their own efforts at renewal? Since all forms of Christian life come from our having the Gospels in our blood, it would seem obvious that an evangelization effort promotes effective renewal in our life. The Gospels not only have inspired the different forms of religious life, but also have helped shape its various expressions and methods. Men and women moved by the Spirit of Christ have gifted the church with at least three prismatic "colors" of Christ-following that look monastic or mendicant or apostolic. The question remains for us today who have been illumined by these various Christ-prisms how our gospel-inspired attitude can reveal the graced mystery of our own lifeform in terms of new depths of meaning and new ways of expression—in the very heritage we claim. The darkness we feel comes not from Jesus, the light-source whom we follow, but from our own self-chosen, squint-eyed angle of vision having so little to do with grace or gospel. So often our efforts at renewal seem more a vain search for one "tree of life" instead of for the God who gives *all* created gifts for our creatively discerned use. Optimism marks the effort of anyone who begins something. Our prayer for ourselves and our church begs again for that grace dear to our God imaged as the prodigal parent who expects the son (and daughter) to be coming up the road—the grace of optimism.

Let Us Pray

**Sing a new song, you faithful,
praise God in the assembly, hallelujah.**

*Sing a new song, you faithful,
praise God in the assembly.
Israel, rejoice in your maker,
Zion, in your king.
Dance in the Lord's name,
sounding harp and tambourine.*

*The Lord delights
in saving a helpless people.
Revel in God's glory,
join in clan by clan.
Shout praise from your throat.
You faithful, this is your glory!*

PSALM 149:1-6, 9

A Spirituality of Communion

As John Paul II closed the holy doors at St. Peter's in Rome on January 6, 2001, the day that the Jubilee of the Year 2000 ended, he issued an apostolic letter titled "At the Beginning of the New Millennium." Similar to the apostolic letter issued in November 1994, "As the Third Millennium Draws Near," this letter challenges all Catholic people in the everyday practice of their faith.

The pope acknowledges that in the first letter it was easy to name specific themes and suggest certain practices as he outlined a program of preparation for us Catholics as we looked towards the new millennium. Now that we are living in the new millennium, it appears more difficult to suggest some sort of schedule for a seemingly unending roll of future years. Not to be daunted, the pope sums up his approach in his call to contemplate the face of Christ, with the manifold ways that this face appears to us in all life's circumstances. He grants that he is not inventing some kind of new program, but rather looking afresh at the program found in the Gospels and in the living tradition of the church.

What receives strong emphasis is the pope's desire for us to make our own a spirituality of communion. This phrase, *spirituality of communion*, the pope had identified in his 1994 apostolic letter, *Vita consecrata*, as describing the mission especially appropriate to members of consecrated-life institutes. No matter the charism that specifies the mission of particular religious lifeforms, the pope had requested that all men and women vowed in consecrated life embrace a spirituality of communion. Religious were encouraged to consciously work at a communion spirituality as an essential part of the gospel spirituality which all share. This spirituality of communion needs to inform their community life and their mission.

By his extension of the call to a spirituality of communion to others, John Paul II has not taken away his invitation to those living the consecrated lifeform to be grounded in a spirituality of communion. Proclaiming now that all Catholics have a responsibility to work at developing this spirituality of communion for our times, the pope underlines a special charge for those vowed in consecrated life to both educate and form others in the Catholic community to understand and live this spirituality of communion. He tells us that this effort will make the church "the home and school of communion." Such creative energy is a spirituality that enhances our awareness of the trinitarian God dwelling within us and embracing us with a divine life of communion. It is a spirituality that makes come alive our realization of the mystical Body in which we see our brothers and sisters truly living a life that is "part of us." It is a spirituality that brings us to see and appreciate the gifts of others not only as gifts from God to them, but also as gifts from God and them to us. It is a spirituality that teaches us how to make room for all our brothers and sisters, so that we truly exclude no one from the table of God our Father and accept what it means to bear one another's burdens. What is so often lacking in the services that are provided secularly (and perhaps we need to examine our own ministries too) is not the actual "body" of services but the "soul" people must put into those services. We must take any "mechanisms" of service and put a soul into them, a soul that gives them full meaning through fullness of communion.

In a postmodern culture, a wise and holy man has proposed linking our Catholic growth in holiness with the special needs of our new millennium. The spirituality of communion he proposes is a privileged and relevant way of imitating Jesus, our incarnate and redeeming Lord.

Let Us Pray

**With joy I heard them say,
"Let us go to the Lord's house."**

*With joy I heard them say,
"Let us go to the Lord's house!"
And now, Jerusalem,
we stand inside your gates.*

*Jerusalem, the city so built
that city and temple are one,
to you the tribes go up,
every tribe of the Lord.*

*It is the law of Israel
to honor God's name.
The seats of law are here,
the thrones of David's line.*

*Pray peace for Jerusalem:
happiness for your homes,
safety inside your walls,
peace in your great houses.*

*For love of family and friends
I say, "Peace be with you!"
For love of the Lord's own house
I pray for your good.*

PSALM 122

The Prism of Dialogue

*L*ife-and-death issues are always with us. At times they touch more poignantly into our experience. Traditionally the November liturgical calendar is associated with death since we begin by remembering all the faithful departed and through the Sunday Eucharists we face somber scripture readings about the end times. December's liturgical calendar, on the other hand, looks more to life, celebrating Mary's conception as the "immaculate one" within a hope-filled Advent season which culminates with the star-bright birth of Jesus our Savior.

Prisms provided by life and death issues have us face the God- and faith-questions in our lives. They are prisms necessary if we are to value realistically who we are, who we are becoming, and what we do, what happens to us. God provides us with many other prisms which help us see and appreciate the everyday richness of our lives and ministries as Christian men and women.

Some people seem to little appreciate that we all use prisms to view life, accept values, and relate to God. Perhaps many of us fail to make use of the variety of prisms available through which to develop a more adequate and vibrant understanding of God, self, church, and world. Rather, some seem to choose to look at life through a single monochromatic lens or through a spattered one that allows only darkness and light and voids the rich subtlety of dawn and sunset beauty.

Christmas presents us with an ever startling prism through which we see God's presence to ourselves and our world. We celebrate God's dialogue with us through the Word by whom all things came into being and in whom we find life. In listening to

John's majestic prologue about the Word becoming flesh, I find the imagery of prisms and of dialogue all of a piece. John Paul II says, "By dialogue we let God be present in our midst; for as we open ourselves in dialogue to one another, we also open ourselves to God." Dialogue—entering into the presence of the Word—is similar to the various prisms of creation which allow us to truly seek and find a laboring God active in our world.

Paul VI, too, had boldly proclaimed that "dialogue is a new way of being church." Drawing upon the imagery of the Word made flesh, he was reclaiming evangelization as an essential element of living the Christian life. Just as some people close themselves from appreciating God's pervasive love that is visible in creation only through a variety of prisms, we can be people closed to the call to be church through dialogue. We can talk only to those people who think exactly as we do. We can read nothing that would challenge or broaden our mind-set. We can enter into conversation not to listen or to learn, but only to accept agreement or refute and "win the day." Not only evangelization, but life itself is being closed down—with others and so with God. It can happen to any of us—bishop, priest, religious, or layperson—who may claim the possession of truth in such a way that dialogue is neither possible nor desired. Every Christmas morn faces us with this question: How do we find the Word in a manger—today? Like shepherds on the watch or like teachable magi, are we available to an alien messenger's voice for direction or to a light from afar to help guide our way?

Pope John Paul II has indicated that dialogue encouraged by the church is fourfold: the dialogue of life found in people's sharing as neighbors, the dialogue of action collaborating for a world more human and more divine, the dialogue of sharing the riches of our spiritual experience and helping one another find the Absolute, the dialogue of specialists exchanging theological insights to deepen understanding and appreciation of religious heritages and spiritual values. No one of us can remain aloof today from at least some aspects of this fourfold dialogue. Dialogue—privileged prisms in our Christian responsibility to be neighbors, ecumenists, and evangelists!

Let Us Pray

**Who can forget God's wonders,
a God, merciful and kind! Hallelujah!**

*With my whole heart
I praise the Lord among the just.
Great are God's works,
a delight to explore.
In splendor, in majesty,
God's justice will stand.*

*Who can forget God's wonders!
a God, merciful and kind
who nourished the faithful,
upheld the covenant,
and revealed mighty deeds,
giving them the land of pagans.*

*Faithful, just, and true
are all God's decrees:
each law in its place,
valid for ever.*

*The Lord redeems the faithful,
decrees a lasting covenant.
Holy and awesome God's name!*

*Fear of the Lord is wisdom's crown,
wise are those who live by it.
Praise the Lord for ever!*

PSALM 111

Prayer: Dialogue for Vocation and Ministry

*W*e Christians come to know our calling to a certain kind of ministry in the church through our fidelity to prayer— a continuing dialogue in our relationship with God. By way of analogy, those in the vocation of married life know that the sacramental celebration of matrimony represents only the *start* of a new relationship together with God. It will take a married lifetime of dialogue with each other and with God and of so living to make the reality of the sacrament come true. Similarly, those in the vocation of religious life signify in some way (commonly through some kind of vow-taking) that they are professing and aiming at a special relationship with God with the wholeness of their lives. Again religious are well aware that vow or profession day is only the beginning of the dialoguing and of the living out of this "aimed-at" relationship. In these vocations of married and religious life, the Christian prayer of both the individual and the community (marital or religious) is a necessary part of the continuing dialogue which keeps alive and nourishes the particular vocation undertaken by our first responding to God's initiative.

The call to minister in the name of Christ and officially authorized in the service of the church also remains grounded in the prayer-dialogue. Ministry, not rooted in prayer, is no ministry at all. Good deeds done may represent admirable humanitarianism which we honor and appreciate, but we do not grace it with the identity of *ministry*. Ministry flows from a consciousness of God and God's ways of acting and from a sense of responsibility for acting in the name of Christ's Body, the church. The pervading consciousness of God and the connatural way of acting as God acts are the fruit of a prayer life, which is consistently fostered "for better, for worse, for richer, for poorer, in sickness and in health." This dialogue permeates and empowers our Christian life as well as our ministry whatever it may be.

In the northern hemisphere, when the summer months are coming to an end, the traditional vacation time is left behind us for another year. We move on to another "work" year and whatever our ministry may be. With the help of God's grace, at this moment and at other "marked" moments, we find ourselves at an opportune time to assess again how our lives, our ministries, and our prayer truly form one healthy and supportive ecological system.

Let Us Pray

My help is the Lord,
who made earth and the heavens.

If I look to the mountains,
will they come to my aid?
My help is the Lord,
who made earth and the heavens.

May God, ever wakeful,
keep you from stumbling;
the guardian of Israel
neither rests nor sleeps.

God shields you,
a protector by your side.
The sun shall not harm you by day
nor the moon at night.

God shelters you from evil,
securing your life.
God watches over you near and far,
now and always.   PSALM 121

Jesus Our Center

What centers our life determines the kind of balance it has. Sometimes we become aware of that center during a quiet prayerful retreat. Perhaps a crisis—the death of someone close to us, a reversal in our own health, a failure in a project, or confusion about future directions—makes us face the question of what centers our lives.

looking for Jesus Christ

True, Jesus Christ is the center of all Christian living. But perhaps all of us need to take stock of our experience of Jesus' centrality to our life and chosen vocation. We find it in our every celebration of the Eucharist, with Jesus as the center in both word and sacrament. We may also find that central Presence in a particular community or an outstanding leader or a special project that helps focus our faith life. Yet such a group or individual or work can also *obscure* what is central to our faith. Perhaps, through no fault of the community or the person or the project, our attention stops at the immediate incarnation of faith in front of us, and these very instruments of grace block out rather than bring us in touch with Jesus Christ. We have heard sad tales of some priest-confessor so antagonizing a penitent, somehow, that the person leaves the confessional in a huff and refuses to actively practice the faith. The person's focus has become fixated on the limited incarnation that each individual priest (or Christian or institution) represents. What Christians take for granted in theory—that Jesus is the center of their faith—can easily be disrupted in practice, amid the trials of living their faith.

With the dearth of vocations to the consecrated life within western Europe and North America today, vocation promoters remind us anew that all of us are limited incarnations of Christ, but we have an important role to play in stirring up and inspiring people to this kind of special following. Still the call remains Christ's, and the focus of a particular ministerial calling is not just one of us nor our church community nor our work; the focus is Jesus, whom we image imperfectly at best. In our own call we can distinguish various influences, but their collective focus is always Jesus.

Our individual crises—like all Christian crises—usually include a loss of our central focus. Again it is individual people, particular communities, and even pet projects that can sometimes stand in the way of our deepening relationship with Jesus. Yes, it is easy to acknowledge that Jesus is the center of lay life, priesthood, and consecrated life—in theory! But in our living of this relationship we often find moments of doubt, confusion, and even anger.

Not only do we experience at times an obscuring of the centrality of Jesus in our personal vocation stories, but we also obfuscate the theology of all Christian vocations by a similar failing. For example, some contemporary studies about consecrated life have little to say about the future of this lifeform because they take no account of its central focus. Without that focus, consecrated life obviously has elements that will be out of balance. As we read some present-day books about religious life's future or as we get involved in various workshops about church ministry, we need to ask ourselves: What centers Catholic or religious life in this way of presenting it? If the consecrated lifeform represented by women and men religious can seem to lose its focus, what are we to say about the whole span of vocations in the church?

The Jesus who is the center of our personal vocation calls for a love relationship. We cannot relate to this Jesus as an abstract concept such as Wisdom, biblically authentic as its personification is. We cannot just identify this Jesus with good actions which we perform in our religious mission: Jesus is more than some category of virtue enhancing human behavior. True, Jesus identifies *with* each person we serve or who serves us, but Jesus has his own identity and his own way of loving and of being loved. Jesus in our lives calls forth from us and from the worshiping community to which we belong the awed response of love he called forth from Thomas: "My Lord and my God!" The mission of our church community or congregation is not identified with making this world a better place to live; our mission as baptized and consecrated people is so related to the Jesus of the Gospels that *together* we make present the actions of Christ. Because of the goodness of a real relationship with Jesus, both as individuals and as communities, we experience that Jesus is the center of our Catholic and religious life, the center of our life-in-mission.

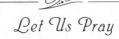

Let Us Pray

To know you is to know life.

All you sheltered by the Most High,
who live in Almighty God's shadow,
say to the Lord, "My refuge, my fortress,
my God in whom I trust!"

"I deliver all who cling to me,
raise the ones who know my name,
answer those who call me,
stand with those in trouble.
These I rescue and honor,
satisfy with long life,
and show my power to save."

PSALM 91:1-2, 14-16

Jesus the Evangelizer

J esus Christ is central to our faith and to its practices. It is good for us to take the time to reflect on how central Jesus is to our life, our prayer, and our work—to our everyday world.

Jesus identified himself as one "preaching the good news." Jesus, first and foremost, proclaimed himself an "evangelizer." He talked about God. He talked about God's sons and daughters. He talked about God's world. Everything Jesus described— the first rays of sunlight, birds nesting, an old woman giving her little bit of money in the temple; whatever he listened to— spring water flowing, a baby's cry, musicians at a wedding feast; things that he could smell and taste—the freshness of a spring rain, the rich flavor of wine; whatever he touched—the mud to put on a blind man's eyes, the coldness of a young man's dead body, the warmth of John's embrace, or the locktight hold of Mary Magdalen on Easter morning: everything spoke to him of the wonder of each of God's creatures, but even deeper down the wonder and beauty of God.

And so Jesus could tell simple stories about seeds and growth, about wedding banquets and joy, about being neighbors and doing good to battered strangers. Every time, in every instance, he is talking about God and our dealings with God.

There is a Latin verb—*conversari*—which means "to turn in relation with" and thus "to interact with," "to have dealings with," "to engage," or "to converse with" (our English word *conversation* obviously derives from it). In the light of this Latin derivation, we might say that all our conversation—all our "talking"—is much broader in meaning and takes in all our dealings with others. Jesus was an evangelizer in all his dealings with the men and women of his time. Every incident in the Gospels is a picture of Jesus evangelizing—engaging people in the divine context of their lives.

What does that say about us as Jesus' followers? To be evangelizers we do not have to go off to school and get degrees in theology. We do not have to exile ourselves to another country. All we need do is deal with the people in our everyday world the way Jesus talked and dealt with the people in his everyday world. He presented to each person a new quality of life; he uncovered divine values beneath the surface of all our human dealings. But for us to act in such a way implies that our world and the events in our lives speak of God to us so that we can speak of God to others. Like Jesus, we have to become aware of a world alive in God. Isn't that an essential to the good news which we live and speak about and deal with others about?

John Paul has stressed repeatedly that we are being called to a new evangelization. Today we call our effort a "new evangelization" because our educated world seems so ignorant of Jesus' way of seeing (seeing deeper down) and because we ourselves, whatever our vocation in life, whatever our age, whatever our talents and education, are newly conscious of our responsibilities to preach the good news. For us to be Christian, to be like Jesus, we must be missionary; we must be evangelizers.

How do we, neophyte evangelizers, start to live in Jesus' world? By reading the Gospels. We need to set an agenda for ourselves of reading the Gospels through—slowly and over and over again. We need to let their words, their stories, become the warp and woof of our lives. We will be imbibing Jesus' way of being an evangelizer. We will assume more and more a stance of dealing with people in Jesus' kind of world—a world alive in God. Like Jesus, we will be doing our part in making ourselves and our world come alive in God. Like Jesus, we will be preaching good news to the "poor," that is, those who have so little a sense of God's presence permeating their everyday world.

Let Us Pray

**How good to sing your love at dawn,
your faithfulness at dusk.**

*How good to thank you, Lord,
to praise your name, Most High,
to sing your love at dawn
your faithfulness at dusk
with sound of lyre and harp,
with music of the lute.
For your work brings delight,
your deeds invite song.*

*The just grow tall like palm trees,
majestic like cedars of Lebanon.
They are planted in the temple courts
and flourish in God's house,
green and heavy with fruit
even in old age.*

*Proclaim that God is just,
my rock without a fault.*

PSALM 92:2-5, 13-16

Experiencing Jesus

*I*n John Paul's apostolic letter "As the Third Millennium Draws Near," the thematic structure of the three-year period 1997-1999 is Trinitarian. Since the distinctly Christological character of the jubilee is a primary emphasis, the first year, 1997, was devoted to "reflection on Christ, the Word of God, made man by the power of the Holy Spirit" (40).

National conferences of bishops, local dioceses and individual parishes, religious congregational provinces, and other church organizations proposed various ways of entering into this reflection on Christ. Some helpful study aids, reflection guides, and discussion outlines were available. Programs and conferences, gatherings among various Christian churches, and especially prayer services took place throughout the year.

We all were called to become a part of this movement—like a three-year-long Advent preparation—to celebrate our Christian jubilee. The challenge for each of us is always accepting our responsibility "to know Christ Jesus" and acting on it. Knowing Jesus was a constant theme of St. Paul's writings to the young churches. It was the theme reemphasized in our preparation for celebrating the millennium. How do we come to know Jesus?

Matthew, Mark, Luke, and John each give us a way of knowing Jesus. Every Gospel account became a composite reflection of the stories told about Jesus within an evangelist's particular community. Details and settings of the same stories differ from Gospel account to Gospel account, and it does not matter. Each way of telling the story is true in its ability to give us an entrance into knowing Jesus. At one moment in our lives,

33

through the Gospel of Mark we may find ourselves impressed by the immediate sense of Jesus' activism, the uncluttered quality of his speech, the directness of his affective response. At another time we appreciate the Jesus of Luke's Gospel, who appears so much the person of prayer, compassion, and lively joy. Sometimes the longer wisdom stories of John's Gospel and the image-identity language of being bread, life, light, vine, shepherd, gate, or paraclete call us to peer deep into our well of meditation. Over and over as we move through the Gospels, we find ourselves always coming to know Jesus.

Perhaps, taking our cue from St. Paul, we might discover anew the insight especially applicable to our growth in knowing Jesus. Necessary and helpful as the Gospel accounts are for our knowing Jesus, only in entering into our own experience will we find the Jesus who calls us by name, knocks at the door of our heart, and persists in bringing about the fullness of the reign of God. St. Paul was marked forever by his experience of One saying to him, "It is Jesus of Nazareth whom you are persecuting." For Paul there was no confusion of James and Joseph and Julia and Claudia with Jesus. But Paul realized that, in his dealings with James and Joseph and Julia and Claudia, he was also dealing with Jesus and coming to know him more. Paul came to know Jesus the more he preached and the more he worked with all the people in his churches and the more he prayed. What Paul focuses for each of us is the Jesus in front of us, the Jesus whose coming we await by the way we live and minister now. Jesus in his total gift of living and dying and Jesus in his sure promise of coming is always being made present to us in the Eucharist and so in his Body, the church. We experience Jesus.

Experiencing Jesus is more than studying Christology or reading the Gospels. Experiencing Jesus is more than serving a soup line or demonstrating for peace. Experiencing Jesus is knowing Jesus in the way that Paul exhorts his churches to know Jesus and to let themselves be seen as models of imitation because of that knowledge. The demand for people who know Jesus in this way has never been so clearly expressed as it is in the pope's apostolic letter. In John's Gospel, the story is told of some Greeks who came forward to Philip, making the request "We want to see Jesus." How will we, with the question coming both from within us and from without, respond to that request?

Let Us Pray

**Search my heart, probe me, God!
Lead me along your ancient way.**

*You search me, Lord, and know me.
Wherever I sit or stand,
you read my inmost thoughts;
whenever I walk or rest,
you know where I have been.*

*Before a word slips from my tongue,
Lord, you know what I will say.
You close in on me,
pressing your hand upon me.
All this overwhelms me —
too much to understand!*

*Where can I hide from you?
How can I escape your presence?
I scale the heavens, you are there!
I plunge to the depths, you are there!*

*If I fly toward the dawn,
or settle across the sea,
even there you take hold of me,
your right hand directs me.*

*If I think night will hide me
and darkness give me cover,
I find darkness is not dark.
For your night shines like day,
darkness and light are one.*

*You created every part of me,
knitting me in my mother's womb.
For such handiwork, I praise you.
Awesome this great wonder!
I see it so clearly!*   PSALM 139:1-14

35

Jesus as Word

We know well the account of the first Pentecost in the Acts of the Apostles. The rush of wind all through the house and the tongues as of fire lighting on each one present recall the thunder and lightning and the fire and clouds as God's presence was made manifest to Moses and the Israelite people at the time of the Sinai covenant. Now the covenant fulfilled in the passion, death, and resurrection of Jesus is confirmed by this new outpouring of God's Spirit.

In the perspective of time dedicated to Jesus Christ, we find that familiar stories can take on fresh meaning. For example, "tongues as of fire" traditionally signify the presence of the Holy Spirit and the gift of preaching the good news, perhaps miraculously even in the many different languages of the crowds addressed on that Pentecost day. Might we also understand by the symbolism of tongue the word of God that each one of us becomes through the gifting of the Spirit?

Jesus as the Word made flesh now joining us together in his risen self brings a new reality to all the baptized as "words of God." Every Christian is a precious and unrepeatable expression of the presence of Christ. All the richness of the Hebrew word *dabar*, translated as both *word* and *deed*, underlies the great hymn which forms the Prologue of the Gospel of St. John. The Word both being God and being in the presence of God, the Word through whom all things came to be and the Word that is the source of life for whatever is, the Word that is a light shining on in the darkness (a darkness that can never overcome the Word)—this Word became flesh "and made his dwelling among us, and we have seen his glory, the glory of an only Son coming from the Father, filled with enduring love" (Jn 1:14).

Jesus as risen Word of God is uniquely the embodied expression of God, acting with all the power and dynamism and love of God. Yet all of us Christians in our own way are not only to be seen as contemporary expressions (presences) of Jesus, but we as word (*dabar*) are also to be active and dynamic (doing deeds)—"love following upon love." The Pentecost tongues as of fire symbolize the action of God speaking us out as images of his son Jesus. We Christians are called to realize anew our responsibility of being expressions of Christ and actions of Christ enfleshed for our world.

But the symbol of the (plural) tongues as of fire also suggests the kind of speaking we describe as *dialogue*. This meaning of the symbol needs strong emphasis in our actions as Christians having entered into a new millennium. Dialogue as conversation does not come easy. In our own day broken marriages, fractured communities, worldwide ethnic and religious violence all attest to the fact. We note from the Pentecost experience that our understanding of dialogue requires a special gifting of the Holy Spirit. Dialogue as a true and necessary element of Christian evangelization requires more than human technique, expertise, and patience. From Paul VI's first encyclical, *Ecclesiam suam*, written in 1964, we become aware of some of the Spirit-filled conditions of dialogue: An esteem for the position of the other side is present, something good in the positions of everyone is preserved, and the possibility not only to enrich others but to be enriched ourselves is retained. *That* is the Christian attitude undergirding our evangelizing dialogue.

Dialogue needs to be a part of our Christian action if we are to be word expressions of Christ. Dialogue starts in our families often torn over values and religious practices; dialogue begins in our religious community, where divisions of traditional and progressive seem to serve two Christs. Dialogue also belongs to an ecumenical-movement effort in our daily dealings with friends and coworkers who worship differently from us or perhaps worship not at all.

We find the kind of dialogue symbolized by the Pentecost tongues only if we are people who are fired by love. The dialogue of evangelization must be modeled after the example of Jesus, the Word of God, the primary Evangelizer. The joy of the risen Jesus as he continues to share his Spirit with his followers needs to make its presence felt in our own desire to dialogue. Then truly tongues as of flame are upon us.

Let Us Pray

The Word was made flesh
and made his dwelling among us.

In the beginning was the Word;
the Word was in God's presence,
and the Word was God.
He was present to God in the beginning.
Through him all things came into being
and apart from him nothing came to be.
Whatever came to be in him, found life,
life for the light of men.
The light shines in the darkness,
a darkness that did not overcome it.

He was in the world,
and through him the world was made,
yet the world did not know who he was.
To his own he came,
yet his own did not accept him.
Any who did accept him
he empowered to become children of God.

The Word became flesh
and made his dwelling among us,
and we have seen his glory:
The glory of an only Son coming from the Father,
filled with enduring love.

JOHN 1:1-5, 10-12, 14

Jesus Crucified

*A*crucifix as a symbol of God's love speaks out a richer and deeper meaning than all the learned and devotional treatises of theologians and mystics. We spend the special liturgical season of Lent allowing the crucified Jesus to touch our lives more closely and to call us to realize a similar willingness to love with all our mind, with all our heart, with all our strength, and with our whole soul.

One of the great wonderments of our Christian Lenten season is the gift to see God in a wholly new way. Philip boldly proposes to Jesus: "Show us the Father and that will be enough for us." And Jesus even more boldly tells Philip: "Whoever has seen me has seen the Father" (Jn 14:8-9). As we look upon the face of the crucified One, we see a face of God never imaged by philosophers. In reasoning to God's existence, we find ourselves caught in a morass of concepts about an all-powerful Being, an impassible Being, a Being far removed from the limitations of our time and space.

Even theologians struggle to hold intact Jesus, the Word made flesh, from his conception to his death and resurrection, through all his experiences of loving, being tempted, learning, enjoying, feeling abandoned, suffering, and dying. But, in looking at a crucifix, we rise above all the somersaults the human mind has to make. We look up and see simply the face of God waiting and loving us with a suffering and compassionate love.

Jesus shows us God looking with love and distress upon so much of our inhumane behavior to one another. He says, "Forgive, they do not know what they are doing." Through

Jesus we see a God who has great desires expressed as "I thirst"—a God who hungers and thirsts for divine justice to permeate our human dealings within families, in workplaces, between nations, so allowing God's glory to shine through. The crucified Jesus helps us to come forward fearlessly before God and plead "Remember me"—for the good that we have done or tried to do, for the pardon that we need, just for the gaze of God's attention. The crucifix allows us to glimpse the face of God's concern, trying to provide support and comfort to all of us Marys and Johns in the midst of our most empty and desolate moments. This is a God who empties Self in each of the gifts presented to us.

Lent's preparatory season for the paschal time provides us with the opportunity to grasp anew the wonder of our Christian understanding of God. Who is this God who has called us into a familial relationship, sharing the very divine life, making us truly brothers and sisters to one another? Who is this God who, waiting patiently in weakness for our love response, gives us further signs of love, each a plea for our attention? Who is this God who labors with us, sometimes the potter, at other times the alert assistant to our own creative actions?

Perhaps we all need to be surprised again that gazing upon the crucifix gives rich insight into our God. Through Jesus, and even more particularly in his crucifixion, we come to know God in intimate ways—ways "hidden from the learned and the clever" and now revealed to us, "the merest children" (Lk 10:21).

To us Jesus says, "Blest are the eyes that see what you see. I tell you, many prophets and kings wished to see what you see but did not see it, and to hear what you hear but did not hear it" (Lk 10:24).

Let Us Pray

**I will not lose hope,
never stop praising you.**

*I will not lose hope,
never stop praising you.*

My lips speak your goodness,
praise each day your saving acts,
though I cannot count them all.
I will enter your palace proclaiming,
"Lord God, you alone are just."

From childhood till now,
you taught me to praise your wonders.
Do not leave me, Lord,
now that I am old.

I can still recount
to a new generation
your power and strength.
Your goodness is boundless,
your works so great;
who can equal you?

You wrack me with torment,
but you give back my life
and raise me from this grave.
You will restore my honor
and wrap me again in mercy.

I will thank you, Lord,
for your true friendship
and play the lyre and harp for you,
to the Holy One of Israel.
I will sing out with joy,
sing of how you saved me.

From morning till night
I will trumpet your goodness;
those who sought my ruin
are defeated and shamed.

PSALM 71:14-24

Prisms for a Christ-Life

Jesus Our Teacher

*Jesus Christ is the beginning and the end, the alpha and the omega,
Lord of the new universe, the great hidden key
to human history and the part we play in it.*
—Paul VI, homily in Manila, 29 November 1970

J esus presents us Christians with two inestimable gifts: familial intimacy with God and a share in divine vision. St. Paul
speaks of God giving us wisdom to understand the mystery, "the
plan he was pleased to decree in Christ, to be carried out in the
fullness of time: namely, to bring all things in the heavens and on
earth into one under Christ's headship" (Ep 1:9-10).
Overwhelmed with the vastness of the vision, we rightly focus on
the gift of intimacy. But, as we come to the end of each liturgical year, we receive reminders about the twinned vision which our
relationship with Jesus entails. The many Gospel incidents of
his curing blindness imply our need for Jesus to give us ever
greater sight along with a deepening love relationship.

One of the Gospel titles which Jesus elicits from us throughout our lives is "Teacher." As we continue to reflect on the
Scriptures and receive graced insight into relationships and
situations of our daily life, we become aware that Jesus remains
our teacher as he was for the people during the time of his public ministry. A teacher provides information, presents new ways
of seeing things, and makes connections with previous experiences, allowing further insights to develop. Through the gift
of the Spirit, Jesus continues giving all the richness of divine
perspective. The Spirit's action gives hope to the church, whose

vision is always in process of renewal. Through the focus of scripture readings during a changeover from Ordinary Time to Advent, the church faces each of us with our personal responsibility to examine whether we continue to deepen our relationship with Jesus and whether we allow Jesus to keep expanding our vision. The question for us: Do we seek out Jesus as our Teacher? If we enter into Matthew's final-judgment scene, how does Jesus find us "seeing" and dealing with our fellow men and women? With our awareness of ecological balance, how responsible are we to an environment given over to our care? Does "all things being created in him" affect our attitude of reverence in exploring Mars or some galaxy in the future?

We talk about "getting stuck in our ways." We sometimes caricature it as a special problem for the older person, but it has no age boundaries. We see children quickly get into certain ritualized ways of playing. We certainly know such patterns in our own behavior. In fact, prejudice is a fixed way of seeing or of relating. In the face of personal and historical evidence, it is a paradox to be engaged in a growing relationship with Jesus and at the same time to cling to prejudice. Does prejudice signal to us that we may be trying to focus myopically on the Jesus relationship without letting Jesus be Teacher for us? We may forget that faith vision is a grace always to be prayed for. Perhaps we have placed ourselves more in the position of Peter refusing to let his feet be washed, and we too need to hear Jesus' reprimand that unless we allow him to wash our feet (that is, allow our relationship with Jesus to affect our way of seeing and of acting) we will end up having no relationship with him. We need to be challenged by the Pauline vision to enter into the divine pleasure of reconciling everything—both on the earth and in the heavens—in Christ.

At the close of a liturgical year, as we listen to the Gospel accounts of end times and final-judgment scenes and then move on, in Advent, to the careful preparations for God's entering into our human history in Jesus, we realize anew how we are called to play our part in the cosmic vision—what St. Paul called "the mystery of Christ," the divine design of salvation. Like St. Paul, we too want to make Christ known, hoping to make every human being complete in Christ, since in him—the image of the invisible God—we see God's image of what it means to be

43

human. And in our Christmas awe we continue to pray that we may have eyes to see that Mystery Incarnate, "the fullness of him who fills the universe in all its parts."

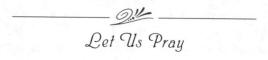

Let Us Pray

I will never stop thanking God,
with constant words of praise.

Come to me, children, listen:
Learn to cherish the Lord.
Do you long for life,
for time to enjoy success?

Keep your tongue from evil,
keep lies far from your lips.
Shun evil, go after good,
press on, seek after peace.

God confronts the wicked
to blot them out for ever,
but turns toward the just
to hear their cry for help.

The troubled call out; God hears,
saves them from all distress.
God stays near broken hearts,
heals the wounded spirit.

The good endure great trials,
but God comes to their rescue
and guards their every bone
so not one is broken.

Evil kills its own kind,
dooms the wicked to death.
God saves those who keep faith;
no trusting soul is doomed.   PSALM 34:12-20

Holy Spirit, Giver of Life

I believe in the Holy Spirit, the Lord, the Giver of life.

The citizens of the United States in recent years have been reinforcing a reputation for being a people that has lost its sense of the sanctity of human life. After a brief lull in the use of the death penalty for what are considered heinous crimes, more and more individual states have been seeking execution for serious crimes committed by both men and women. Then, when we look to the beginning of life, we find that abortion in the United States, even in late term, is justified through the most permissive legal understanding allowed by any Western nation. Finally, when we consider the possible end of life, assisted suicide for the elderly or for the chronically ill is already legal in one state and is being promoted by a number of people who defend what is euphemistically called "mercy killing." As we entered into the new millennium, this most powerful, prosperous, and well-educated nation was sadly being identified as a people that readily "takes life."

It is good for us to focus upon the Holy Spirit as we move into the third millennium guided by the pastoral plan, "As the Third Millennium Draws Near," presented to us by Pope John Paul. Whatever the strength of our faith, the Holy Spirit is the Trinitarian Person most difficult for us to talk about, to imagine,

looking for the spirit

45

and to relate to. *Spirit, breath, wind, love, fire* are words that in themselves have no face nor even a substance that can be grasped. And yet these are some of the common, traditional words applied to the One we call the Third Person of our Trinitarian God. We might, though, begin by calling in prayer upon the Spirit by a name appropriate to the times in which we live.

In the Nicene Creed we express our belief in the Person called the Holy Spirit, professing first that he is Lord God and then designating this Person as "the Giver of life." What a wonderful identity—Giver of life—especially in regard to a people earning a reputation as "takers of life." It seems obvious that a basic gift we seek from God is a renewed reverence, respect, and appreciation for human life.

Perhaps we all need an examination of conscience on behavior involving us as "takers of life." "Takers of life" can involve an attitude which sullies our approach to any part of God's creation—each part a gift from God. We can become so self-centered that everything—from the ecological environment to the earth's resources to human life itself—is viewed in its value *now* for us. Takers of life know no gratitude, for life is not seen in terms of gifting but only in terms of getting, a disease of a consumer society. Let us pray that the Holy Spirit will inspire and guide our efforts to be, like God, givers of life. The age-old prayer still speaks out our desire: "Come, Holy Spirit, fill the hearts of your faithful."

Let Us Pray

Lord, be my guide.

The Lord is my shepherd,
I need nothing more.
You give me rest in green meadows,
setting me near calm waters,
where you revive my spirit.

You guide me along sure paths,
you are true to your name.
Though I should walk in death's dark valley,
I fear no evil with you by my side,
your shepherd's staff to comfort me.

You spread a table before me
as my foes look on.
You soothe my head with oil;
my cup is more than full.

Goodness and love will tend me
every day of my life.
I will dwell in the house of the Lord
as long as I shall live.

PSALM 23

Holy Spirit as Paraclete

*W*hen Pope John Paul identified a millennium preparation time especially focused on the Holy Spirit and his sanctifying presence within the community of Christ's disciples, he did not make use of the word *paraclete* as a special identity-word for the Spirit. Yet this strange-sounding word *paraclete* holds meanings particularly appropriate for our Christian understanding of God.

The word *paraclete* becomes a kind of prism when it is used as a title for the Holy Spirit. Often in the English-language translations of the Gospel of St. John *paraclete* is retained as a direct transliteration of the Greek word, literally meaning "one called alongside of." The first meaning favored in a reading of the Johannine Gospel is that of a *defender*, signifying someone like a defense attorney in a lawsuit. At other times the meaning is broadened by the translation of *counselor*, as in one who carefully listens and gives clarity and advice and support. Still another meaning which is frequently found is captured in the word *comforter*. A comforter is one who strengthens and upholds. *Paraclete*, then, can be viewed differently, depending upon the plane of reflection, but all the meanings are rich in connotation for us as recipients of this personal paschal gifting of Christ.

The church season of Lent provides us with the occasion to acknowledge ourselves as sinners in the presence of a just and compassionate God. But the Spirit as paraclete presents us with an image of God as the one who is the "defending lawyer"—the one who is spending his energies defending us, in the face of any accusers we might have. God the Spirit is the one who gives this sense of divine presence as defender. As St. Paul would reflect, "If God is for us, who can be against us?" (Rm 8:31).

Lent is also a time for us to seek counsel and assess the drives and ambitions, the values and the dreams, that fill and motivate our life. Discernment of spirits in the decision making that structures our lives is a gift of the Spirit to all the members of the Christian community. A Vatican II church, trying to live out its agenda described in the Pastoral Constitution on the Church in the Modern World, has great need to call upon the discernment gift of the Counselor. We know that, in the some-time darkness of our attempt to live a Christian life in a world of differing values, our refuge is in seeking the counsel of a God so involved with us that his person is experienced as one who enlightens and guides. All too often we act fearfully or rashly, with little reliance on Christ's promise: "In that hour, say what you are inspired to say. It will not be yourselves speaking but the Holy Spirit" (Mk 13:11).

Lent uncovers our weakness and fragility in our following of Christ. We, like the first apostles, are too ready to yield or take flight in the face of temptation or opposition. Our actions do speak louder than our words, and to the eyes of secular society we might appear even to deny our faith. God enters into our lives at these times with the support and strength necessary for our Christian witness. We come to recognize our God especially as the one who confirms and consoles. "By patient endurance you will save your lives" (Lk 21:19).

In John's Gospel, Jesus describes the giving of the Spirit in terms of an abiding presence of "another" paraclete with us. In his Last Supper discourse, Jesus first applies the title to himself by his using the word *another*, and then through the rest of the discourse he gives *Paraclete* over to the Holy Spirit as a proper name. The Spirit makes real to our human experience that God's presence is truly that of *paraclete*—one who defends, one who counsels, and one who strengthens. Jesus, the pioneer for our faith life, inspires our confidence in such a God.

Lent is the traditional time in the church for a renewed effort in our following Christ in the pattern of his paschal mystery. We, like Jesus, can only walk the road to Jerusalem if we are led by the Spirit. As we enter into the 21st-century era with a renewed emphasis upon our evangelization efforts, we need to call upon God, who is truly *Paraclete* for us.

Let Us Pray

**God, you are the fount of life,
you give us light and we see.**

*Your mercy, Lord, spans the sky;
your faithfulness soars among the clouds.
Your integrity towers like a mountain;
your justice runs deeper than the sea.
Lord, you embrace all life:
How we prize your tender mercy!*

*God, your people seek shelter,
safe in the warmth of your wings.
They feast at your full table,
slake their thirst in your cool stream,
for you are the fount of life,
you give us light and we see.*

PSALM 36:6-10

Holy Spirit,
Sign of God's Ownership

The Spirit is God's mark of ownership on you.

O nce, on a visit to South Africa, I noticed how often automobiles have distinguishing numbers, letters, or symbols painted boldly on their doors and even on their rooftops. I came to realize that these signs are not just expressions of beauty or individuality, but they provide a visible way of claiming ownership and discouraging carjacking or thievery.

St. Paul exhorted the members of his Christian communities to rejoice because the Spirit is God's mark of ownership over them. As we celebrate Pentecost in our church year, we may have a certain longing for tongues of fire as a vivid experience of the Spirit's presence and power in our lives. But I wonder whether today we in the Christian community seize the opportunity to welcome the gripping—though commonplace—idea of the Spirit as God's ownership. We own things, but we do not like to think of ourselves as being owned, even by God. We want to think of ourselves as autonomous, free, in charge of our own fate. Sometimes, though, we may admit to ourselves how much we have bought into (or, perhaps more correctly, "been bought by") the values of our culture, the prejudices of our ethnic groups, and the political assumptions of our times. We are likely owned in many more ways than we care to discover—and we may show it by the way we live! Perhaps, then, we need to work at making our lives belong more visibly to God.

Our Pentecost experience may not include rushing wind or fiery tongues, but the presence of the Spirit in our lives is still meant to be—as in Paul's communities—the mark of God's ownership. Sometimes we too facilely identify the church as a hierarchical church or, more in vogue today, a church of the laity. But the truest reality is that the church is one people assembled, all belonging to the Spirit, marked with God's ownership. Living this reality consciously must be part of our personal effort. Our personal witnessing of this reality is central to our evangelizing efforts, more necessary in the secularizing trends of our times than in Paul's Roman Empire days.

What does God's ownership mean for us? God's ownership of us, marked by the presence of the Spirit in our lives, is meant to shine out in our way of acting. The traditional expression is "giving glory to God." Giving glory means that we become transparent enough that God and God's life and God's love can shine out through us. For example—to draw from the everyday behaviors suggested by St. Paul—the way we talk. St. Paul stresses that a person marked by the Spirit speaks only helpful words, words that build up and provide for what is needed. It is how Jesus speaks. What we say should do good for those who hear us. Beyond our words, what can distinguish our dealings with people—the occasions for God's glory to shine out in us—is our kindness and our readiness to forgive. It is how Jesus acted.

At a time in our world when massacres of Christians by Christians take place in Rwanda and Burundi, when fellow Christians seek revenge for age-old wrongs in Northern Ireland, when Orthodox, Catholic, and Muslim (all believers in the one God) slaughter one another in ethnic feuds, we can rightly wonder about our welcoming God's Spirit as a mark of God's ownership over us. But let us look into our own mirrors. When everyday human interaction includes ourselves as automobile drivers whose road rage leads us to endanger others, when we "good people" continue to flee from neighborhoods that are in the process of racial integration, when we find ourselves hardened to the reality of abortion and assisted suicide, we can question whether we as individuals and as communities have allowed the Spirit enough welcome to dwell within us, whether God's ownership of us shines out.

In an engaging childlike way, St. Paul exhorted the early Christians not to make the Spirit sad. We need to assess whether our Christian living shows forth God's ownership. Or do we make the Spirit sad?

Let Us Pray

**Whoever has integrity
shall climb the mountain of God.**

*God owns this planet
and all its riches.
The earth and every creature
belong to God.*

*God set the land on top of the seas
and anchored it in the deep.*

*Who is fit to climb God's mountain
and stand in his holy place?*

*Whoever has integrity:
not chasing shadows,
not living lies.*

*God will bless them,
their savior will bring justice.
These people long to see the Lord,
they seek the face of Jacob's God.*

PSALM 24:1-6

The Spirit and Forgiveness

Receive the Holy Spirit. Whose sins you shall forgive . . .

One of the most moving moments for me during a meeting with women and men religious in Johannesburg, South Africa, had to do with forgiveness and reconciliation. One of the participants, an Augustinian novice director, observed that, just as the government had set up a Truth and Reconciliation Commission to bring a certain peaceful closure to the painful memories of the apartheid era, so it might be helpful in the church and in our various religious congregations to establish a similar kind of commission. He noted: "The differences in policies and practices among whites, coloreds, and blacks—in our memberships and in our ministries, not just between parish congregations but even within a single province of women or men religious—have caused pain and left scars that a church or religious-life truth and reconciliation commission might go a long way to healing." A deeply reflective silence followed, and then a chorus of voices began to express a universal agreement among the white, colored, and black religious present that this agenda needed to be pursued in future meetings among the conference members.

Our life experience tells us that we human beings do not easily come to forgiveness and reconciliation. We even find the gift of forgiveness by God the most difficult of God's many gifts for us to accept. Commonly we try to earn forgiveness; we attempt to "make up" for whatever we have done badly or left undone. Our behavior is just as consistent in our relations with one another as it is with God. It is often evident in the way we offer forgiveness: on the condition that the person—whether it is my brother or sister, my son or daughter, my friend or fellow worker—performs in a way to deserve it. And yet forgiveness is just *that*: a gift "given for" someone.

Jesus made it clear through his parables and his example that forgiveness is first a gift from God—given for us—and then God invites us into sharing the gift by the way we live. God so much wanted us to share in the divine way of acting that, in the prayer that Jesus taught, it is the only petition to which our personal actions are connected: "Forgive us our sins as we forgive those who sin against us." Forgiveness is so far beyond our ordinary human capacities, Jesus seems to indicate, that we need to pray for the gift in every "Our Father" we say.

On that first Easter Sunday evening, Jesus appears to his disciples—all locked up in fear—and offers first for their peace the gift of his Spirit. With the permanent gifting of the Holy Spirit comes the power for us to forgive. The church for centuries has seen in these very words the foundation of the sacrament of reconciliation. But, long before the sacramental system was clearly delineated, the church understood the gifting of the Spirit and the power to forgive as an essential part of our Christian living in peace. Like Jesus, we are meant to stand ready always to forgive. The old proverb "To err is human, to forgive divine" is very true. Even with the baptismal and confirmation gift of the Spirit, we more often feel weighted by our human meanness than moved by divine forgiveness.

At first we might be inclined to think of forgiveness as being about the past. But, just as the Truth and Reconciliation Commission may be recalling past happenings only to look towards the future of South African society, so God's forgiveness of us and our forgiveness of one another always look toward the future—the way we will relate and the way we will act. That is why, as we seek to grow in our spiritual life, we need to invoke the Spirit. For our world of age-old hatreds and fresh hurts cries out for us Christians to give witness to the precious gift of forgiveness. Giving witness to forgiveness—*that* will be our new evangelization.

Let Us Pray

You welcome a changed heart, O God.

Creator, reshape my heart,
God, steady my spirit.
Do not cast me aside
stripped of your holy spirit.

Save me, bring back my joy,
support me, strengthen my will.
Then I will teach your way
and sinners will turn to you.

Help me, stop my tears,
and I will sing your goodness.
Lord, give me words
and I will shout your praise.

When I offer a holocaust,
the gift does not please you.
So I offer my shattered spirit;
a changed heart you welcome.

PSALM 51:12-19

The Spirit and Unity

That they may be one, as we are one . . .

*P*ope John Paul II wrote the encyclical *That They May Be One (Ut Unum Sint)* in 1995. This document, dealing with our Christian commitment to ecumenism, took its title from the petition spoken by Jesus in his Last Supper discourse as remembered in the Gospel of St. John. Jesus prayed that all his followers would be blessed with the unity, the oneness which his Abba-Father and he enjoyed: "That all may be one as you, Father, are in me, and I in you; I pray that they may be one in us" (Jn 17:21).

A most pervasive tendency among us is to make a division of any grouping into "them" and "us." It happens in families, between those siblings or relatives who are "out" and those who are "in." It occurs in the way male and female differences have become "them" and "us" in the gender movements of our day. It is evident in the struggles caused by racial, ethnic, or religious distinctions. Witness our contemporary history of the United States, Bosnia, Sudan, and Rwanda. It is found in the church whether between hierarchy/clergy and laity or between liberal and conservative/traditionalist. Even an official church action like excommunication pronounced by local bishops or by Vatican congregations seems to divide off members into a "them" against an "us." Historically it has been true that religious congregations vied with each other within the church, for example, the competition between branches of 14th-century Franciscans and between 17th-century Dominicans and Jesuits—

something in consecrated life, thank the Spirit, which seems less a problem in our time. It is writ large in the struggles in our economic world between east and west and between north and south—the "have's and the have-not's." The "them" and "us" (or, at its personal ultimate, "the world" and "me") mentality seems to be in the very air we breathe.

One desire that should be a constant in our life is that the Spirit gift us with various prisms through which to view life and our relationships with others in more accepting ways. We might pray that the Spirit become for us the pervading atmosphere in which we live and move and have our being. We need to stir ourselves to take the first few steps away from "political maps" that divide everything into a "them" and "us." We could decide to take action by our daily examination of conscience. We begin our examen by thanking God for the small ways in which we have allowed the Spirit to unite ourselves with others in our thinking about them and in our acting towards them. We then examine ourselves and note the occasions when we have succeeded in avoiding a "them" and "us" attitude and the occasions when we have not. We, moved by the Spirit, beg God's forgiveness for the obtuseness of our minds and the hardness of our hearts in choosing and reinforcing the deadly worldview of division in our behaviors of this day. Finally we ask ever more fervently for the outpouring of the Spirit upon us to strengthen us in our mission. Empowered by the Spirit, we dedicate ourselves anew to struggle at eliminating the "them" and "us" mentality in our family, in our community, in our parish life, in our work life, and in whatever other areas it seems to prevail.

The Spirit is the Love-Reality, the very *communio*, of God's life. The Spirit, we might say, is the Love-touch of God's life in us, and so the Spirit's presence in our lives means our communion of life with our Trinitarian God. The Spirit's activity is God's creating the *communio* among all of us here and now. Christ's prayer, then, becomes more insistently our prayer and moves us so to work to bring about a world that is at once more human and more divine—that all may be one.

Let Us Pray

All praise is yours, God in Zion.

Praise is yours, God in Zion.
Now is the moment
to keep our vow,
for you, God, are listening.

All people come to you
bringing their shameful deeds.
You free us from guilt,
from overwhelming sin.

Happy are those you invite
and then welcome to your courts.
Fill us with the plenty of your house,
the holiness of your temple.

You give victory
in answer to our prayer.
You inspire awe, God, our savior,
hope of distant lands and waters.

Clothed in power,
you steady the mountains;
you still the roaring seas,
restless waves, raging nations.
People everywhere
stand amazed at what you do,
east and west shout for joy.

PSALM 65:1-9

Prisms for a Christ-Life

Holy Spirit as Gift Gifting

The imagery of the Holy Spirit as an iconographer holds an age-old place in the tradition of the Eastern churches. The Holy Spirit is painting us in the image and likeness of God. But, of course, we acknowledge Jesus Christ as the image of the invisible God (Col 1:15). Consequently, in working with us as a painter does with an icon, the Holy Spirit continues throughout our life to bring out in us another face of Jesus.

When we enter the Advent preparation for Christmas, this way of understanding our relationship to the Spirit seems especially appropriate. The Holy Spirit is always laboring to bring to birth within us a fuller identity with Jesus. Our life can be understood as an Advent season in which we are being prepared over the span of our earthly life for the reality of our life-with-God forever in Christ. At the same time, from our meditation upon the Gospels and from our following in Christ's footsteps, our daily life can be seen as one spent living in imitation of the hidden and public life of Jesus. With every stroke of his painter's brush, the Spirit inspires, encourages, and strengthens us to live "like Jesus," to live as Christ-ians. For the Spirit, according to Jesus' promise, is the one who "remains" with us, the one who will "be within" us (Jn 14:17).

From the Gospel of St. John, we learn that the Holy Spirit is a gift to us—Jesus' gift to us of "another Paraclete" (that is, one who functions just like Jesus himself, who is our first Paraclete) or, perhaps stated with more theological precision, a gift from the "us" of Father and Son. Fumblingly struggling to say something about the identity and life of our triune God, our theological tradition at times expresses it in this way: The Father gives himself over fully to the Son, and the Son gives himself over fully to the Father, and the fullness of the Love shared between them is a Gift-Person, a Love-Person. As a result, our Trinitarian God is caught up in a life of relationship, of total giving, of total sharing—a God who is Love, a God who is all Gift.

The Spirit, whose very relational identity within the Trinity is Gift and Love, plays this same role in God's outreach to creation—for example, the imagery of the brooding of Spirit over the waters of creation and the Spirit's overshadowing of Mary in the annunciation scene. From revelation and from our experience, we know that God relates to us through all of creation as "gifts"—gifts that are meant to help us to know, to love, and to serve God by our proper appreciation and use of these gifts. God relates to us through Jesus as gift of identity with us as human. Jesus is called the new Adam because we human beings in the Jesus-Gift have become truly new and original. God relates to us in baptism, confirmation, and all the sacraments and sacramentals of our Christian life in the gift of the one we call the Holy Spirit. The process of our growing in grace or, as the Eastern churches say it more daringly, the process of our divinization continues as God's Spirit-Gift stays with us. We Christians, made newly human in Christ, have come to understand God in a new and original way: a triune God, a Gift-God, a God of Love.

At Christmas, then, we see again, with eyes of faith, God's gift of identity with us through Jesus. Year after year, all the wonder of this gift seen and remembered as a baby fills the heights and depths of our soul. But, when we reflect on the Spirit in our life, we recall anew, especially in this Christmas season, how much the Holy Spirit—God-Gift—keeps giving us the way to be Christ for our times. We pray to the Spirit to bring forth more fully in us the icon of Jesus each of us is created to be—made in the image and likeness of God.

Let Us Pray

**I look to you, O God,
to be my strength this day, hallelujah.**

*God, my God, you I crave;
my soul thirsts for you,
my body aches for you
like a dry and weary land.
Let me gaze on you in your temple:
a vision of strength and glory.*

*Your love is better than life,
my speech is full of praise.
I give you a lifetime of worship,
my hands raised in your name.
I feast at a rich table,
my lips sing of your glory.*

*On my bed I lie awake,
your memory fills the night.
You have been my help,
I rejoice beneath your wings.
Yes, I cling to you,
your right hand holds me fast.*

PSALM 63:2-9

The Father Face of God

Whoever has seen me has seen the Father.
—John 14:9

We can talk about God in some very un-Christian ways. As we "dress up" God in the various cultural and time-bound categories of our human world, we are inevitably limited, in both our reasoning and our imagining. When we get swept up into a highly intellectualized philosophical approach, we find ourselves projecting a vague, abstract, and sometimes frightening power and a childishly understood world. God without a face.

Although Jesus lived within human limitations of time and culture, he dared to speak "with authority" about the reign of God in images and parables that tore down the temple curtain of separation to let people catch some glimpses of God that are new. The synoptic Gospels—Mark, Matthew, and Luke—talk of a celebratory invitation to a banquet, of a shepherd doggedly searching out a lost sheep, so that we come to know and relate to God with fresh affective response. But the Gospel of St. John stands out as the Gospel of the God revealed to us by Jesus as "Father."

Few are the chapters in John's Gospel that do not have explicit reference to God as Father. The qualities of this Father-God tumble out. This God is the God of life: "Just as the Father who has life sent me and I have life because of the Father ..." (Jn 6:44). This is

63

a God who works: "My Father is at work until now, and I am at work as well" (Jn 5:17). This is a God who teaches: "My doctrine is not my own; it comes from him who sent me" (Jn 7:16); "I say only what the Father has taught me" (Jn 8:28). This is a God who cultivates growth: "I am the true vine, and my Father is the vinegrower" (Jn 15:1). Above all, this God is the one who loves: "The Father loves the Son and has given everything over to him" (Jn 3:35); "the one who loves me will be loved by my Father" (Jn 14:21).

In retreat notes published as a book, *The Ignatian Exercises in the Light of St. John*, Cardinal Carlo Maria Martini SJ reflects that a way of considering the Fourth Gospel is to see it as a gospel of prayer. It is prayer not just from people responding to Jesus as we do so often in our prayer lives, but prayer also from Jesus to the one he lovingly calls Abba-Father. From Jesus we learn how we are meant to grow in our relationship with God. And so this Gospel, in teaching a way of relating to God for the mature Christian, is paradoxically the Gospel most insistent in reminding us that we are still "children" who have—and who need for our very existence—a Father.

We are called, in imitation of Jesus, to relate to a God from whom we have everything—all that we are and all that we would call "our own." This is the God that Jesus describes as the One apart from whose words he himself has nothing to say, the God apart from whose works he has no work to do. As Christian evangelizers, then, we need to follow the example of Jesus so that what we say flows from our union with this God. As Christian ministers we need to strive that all our deeds and good works flow from the baptismal grace given by God that makes us all very special children, God's sons and daughters. It is from this God we have come—a Source we call by Jesus' word Father—and it is to this God we direct our whole life as the One we, with John, identify as Love.

If we let the words of St. John enter more deeply into our very being, we will find ourselves being shaped and molded by the reality behind our personally limited understandings of God as Father and God as Love. This is the revealed God of Scripture we seek to know and make known

Let Us Pray

Favor and bless us, Lord.
Let your face shine on us.

Favor and bless us, Lord.
Let your face shine on us,
revealing your way to all peoples,
salvation the world over.

Let nations sing your praise,
every nation on earth.

The world will shout for joy,
for you rule the planet with justice.
In fairness you govern the nations
and guide the people of earth.

Let the nations sing your praise,
every nation on earth.

The land delivers its harvest,
God, our God, has blessed us.
O God, continue your blessing,
may the whole world worship you.

PSALM 67

God the Father Metaphor

How are we to speak of God the Father at a time when we desire to be more sensitive about sexist phrases and patriarchal soundings? The male imaging of God, both in our theology study and in our liturgical services, has come under criticism from many Christians, often stimulated by the ground-breaking work of feminist theologians—no matter that Jesus referred most often to God as Father (though he also used other image words or examples, of course, including feminine ones). Although the Hebrew word *Abba* is used only once in the Greek Gospels—in Mark—and seldom in Paul's epistles, the significant intimacy of this word (and its relevance to Jesus' teaching the prayer "Our Father") has made it central to the Christian understanding of the relationship of ourselves to God—One upon whom we can call, by our being baptized into Jesus, with his love-word *Abba*.

God, for us Christians, is above all personal. We talk to God as a person. In our everyday life we learn early on to call out to "Mom" and "Dad," but we do not find ourselves saying "O Parent." Parent, much as it blends masculine and feminine, is not used in personal address. So parent and other ways of avoiding the Jesus-chosen name "Father" do not tend to keep us true to our Christian faith. Nor is it helpful to use activity names in our sharing in the trinitarian life since all God's activities outside the Trinity are the work of the one God. In addition, the activity titles of creator, redeemer, and sanctifier are not the warm personal words that elicit and express a love-response on our part.

Father Walter Ong SJ, a scholar in language expression, in his book *Fighting for Life*, makes a helpful observation about how appropriate the use of the Father word is for God. The father metaphor seems more apt for God even than a mother metaphor because of the very way that God relates to us. A mother in carrying a child in her womb for nine months knows well the meaning of "bone of my bones and flesh of my flesh." In ordinary circumstances, a mother knows and feels how much this child (baby) belongs to her. A father's experience is necessarily different. A father must lay claim to a child. Leaving aside our contemporary scientific DNA testing for paternity, a father has to step forward and begin the bonding process with a baby boy or girl whom he believes is, and accepts as, the one he "fathered."

We Christians understand that God steps forward and, in and through Jesus the Christ, claims us as his children. We are "daughters and sons of God," albeit "adopted" because Jesus alone merits the title "the only-begotten Son." True, we are God's creation, but we are not of the "substance" (like "bone of my bones and flesh of my flesh") of God. We are claimed by God in Jesus; we are adopted. The gospel metaphor of Father, then, in a transcendent way of choosing and claiming, has given us the relationship we rejoice in—daughters and sons who right-fully call upon God with Jesus' word Abba. God expends great energy all our life long to convince us that we are beloved ones. Perhaps we glimpse the importance of God's choosing us as beloved in Christ when we consider the criteria of the apostle. When the Eleven were considering how to fill the place of Judas after the resurrection and ascension of Jesus, they used the criterion of having been present from the time of Jesus' bap-tism by John at the Jordan. For all of us followers of Jesus, he shares with us in our baptism what had been the consolation of his own in the Jordan event. We are taken into the circle of God's inner life of trinitarian love.

Our consideration of God as Father helps us appreciate more fully the graced relationship which we Christians, through Jesus Christ and our Scriptures and tradition, have been given the privilege of understanding—along with the happy respon-sibility of making our response. In balancing our images of God after the manner of Jesus, we Christians hold fast to the fact that what gifts us is our way of praying to God as "Our Father."

Let Us Pray

God determined out of love
to adopt us through Jesus Christ.

Bless God, the Father of our Lord Jesus Christ,
who blessed us from heaven through Christ
with every blessing of the spirit.

Before laying the world's foundation,
God chose us in Christ
to live a pure and holy life.

God determined out of love
to adopt us through Jesus Christ
for the praise and glory of that grace
granted us in the beloved.

By Christ's blood we were redeemed,
our sins forgiven
through extravagant love.

With perfect wisdom and insight
God freely displayed the mystery
of what was always intended:
a plan for the fullness of time
to unite the entire universe through Christ.

EPHESIANS 1:3-10

Praying the Our Father

When we pray to God, we would do well to bring into sharper focus to whom we pray. For the sake of our prayer life, we might examine how our praying is shaped by Jesus' teaching the Our Father. What are the ordinary elements that we as Christ's disciples appropriately bring to our day-to-day way of praying?

Our Father

Our prayer begins with our, not my, "hello" to One who has loved us into life, the One we call upon as the "God of our life," "Giver of all good gifts," "Abba" (Jesus' love-word).

who art in heaven

One so close, so totally present to us, and yet not in the world of our control—beyond the sphere of limitation and death.

hallowed be thy name

You are holy—totally other than us; you are God, and we are not. It is your world; we are your creation. Awe-filled, we say "Holy your name!"

thy kingdom come

For us and for the world, we want what you want. Why? because it is out of love you create and you act and you seek out.

thy will be done on earth as it is in heaven

May your desires become our desires and so let us act with you—as ones who love.

69

give us this day our daily bread
> Daily let us be with you and work with you for all that sustains our life with you.

and forgive us our trespasses
as we forgive those who trespass against us
> There are times we pay no heed to you; we become so caught up in our own way of finding life and in our own way of seeking love. Forgive us for receiving your love so awkwardly, sometimes so grudgingly. Help us to act like you in offering forgiveness to others who hurt us in any way.

and lead us not into temptation
> You know our limits; please be gentle with us in your unquenchable love. Even more we ask you to be strong within us as together we face the things that might make us less than the human persons you call us to be.

but deliver us from evil
> We know that you are always a saving God, and we stand always in your presence as ones who need saving—so we believe, so we trust, so we love.

Moved by Christ's Spirit, our praying may take shape in any and all of these reflections of Jesus' way of teaching us to pray. So we pray in Jesus' name.

Let Us Pray

**Father, Lord of heaven and earth,
to you I offer praise.**

On one occasion Jesus spoke thus:
Father, Lord of heaven and earth,
to you I offer praise;
for what you have hidden from the learned and clever
you have revealed to the merest children.
Father, it is true.

You have graciously willed it so.
Everything has been given over to me by my Father.
No one knows the Son but the Father,
and no one knows the Father but the Son—
and anyone to whom the Son wishes to reveal him.
Come to me, all you who are weary and find life burdensome,
and I will refresh you.
Take my yoke upon your shoulders and learn from me,
for I am gentle and humble of heart.
Your souls will find rest,
for my yoke is easy and my burden light.

MATTHEW 11:25-30

The Prodigal Father

*M*any of us are familiar with the late Henri Nouwen's *Return of the Prodigal Son*—a book in which Nouwen reflects on the Gospel story and Rembrandt's painting of the same title displayed in the Hermitage museum in Saint Petersburg in Russia. Some years after writing the book, Nouwen died while he was on a journey to Russia to participate in a television feature dealing with the painting and his book.

Nouwen's fascination with Rembrandt's painting of the famous Lucan parable makes a special appeal to us. In the directions of Pope John Paul's apostolic letter "As the Third Millennium Draws Near," we know that the year 1999 was dedicated to seeing things "in the perspective of Christ: in the perspective of the 'Father who is in heaven'" (§49; Mt 5:45). Just as the previous two years were dedicated respectively to Jesus Christ and to the Holy Spirit, so this final year preparatory to the new millennium was focused particularly upon God—the One Jesus calls Abba-Father.

A dynamic is uniquely associated with the final year of the second millennium. It is the journey motif. We are to pay special attention to the fact that we human beings are "on the journey to the house of the Father." The God we come to know on our journeying is not just a good God but a God of forgiving love, a compassionate God. Following an allusion made by the pope, we might identify the year 1999 as the year of the parable of the prodigal. Like the prodigal, we all are on the road leading home. Like the prodigal, we may have a mix of feelings about the life choices we have made and the values we have lived. Like the prodigal, in the midst of evaluating our life we sometimes find ourselves needing to throw ourselves on God's mercy—and ready to do so. In one way or another, then, we tend to find ourselves on the road with the prodigal, similar in our rueful disquiet about past failings and in our modest plans for a fresh start. Most important, though, is our coming to the ever new and deepening understanding of the reality of God's relationship with us—the One who keeps watching for us whenever our approach, the One who hastens to embrace us into the family.

Demanding as the actual journeying of our life may be, our attention should be fixed primarily on the journey of our heart. The heart needs to be quiet and hear the questions: Where are we now in our journey? Is life for us Christians lived truly as a pilgrimage—a journey with a direction? How have we come to know God in our adult years? Is God the one we experience as so compassionate to us that we feel the pull to address God with Jesus' intimacy-of-love word Abba?

Most commonly, pilgrimage evokes a picturing of a group moving onward together. So, too, in our pilgrimage we are not alone. Our Christian community in all its various forms—family, parish, sodality, religious congregation—makes real that it is a "we" journeying together to the Father. The call to a new evangelization summons us, already known in Pauline times as a people of "The Way," to be welcoming to a humanity searching for the way.

Pilgrims are known to tell stories as in Chaucer's Canterbury Tales, and pilgrims are known to sing songs as the psalms so often describe. As we continue our journeying, we need to tell one another our own parables of a pilgrimage home. Together we sing songs of praise to the Father, "who has blessed us in Christ with every spiritual blessing" (Ep 1:3-4). Every year can be a special pilgrimage for us all.

Let Us Pray

**I look for your face, O God,
I beg you not to hide.**

*O God, listen to me;
be gracious, answer me.
Deep within me a voice says,
"Look for the face of God!"*

*So I look for your face,
I beg you not to hide.
Do not shut me out in anger,
help me instead.*

*Do not abandon or desert me,
my savior, my God.
If my parents rejected me,
still God would take me in.*

PSALM 27:7-14

God's Reign

Thy kingdom come.

The words kingdom and reign sound off-putting to most Americans. We have little tradition of kings and queens. What we have of it stems from a relatively brief past of early colonizers looking back to European roots. But, when we Christians pray the Lord's prayer, we find ourselves begging God—the one we address by Jesus' word Father—that "your kingdom will come." By Jesus' teaching us a way to pray as he prays, we seem to be using language that pictures God as ruler or king and God's area of influence as a kingdom.

What do we mean when we pray "Thy kingdom come"? Perhaps we can gain some clarity by identifying first what we do not mean. Kingdom is not to be identified with any political entity. Even the age-old notion of Christendom was not the same as this kingdom, and so the breakup of Christendom was not a dissolution of the kingdom. Kingdom is not a certain physical locale.

The Roman Catholic Church as an institutional structure is not identified with the kingdom. The church has an important role to play in the kingdom, but it is not the kingdom itself. The church continues the mission of Jesus in proclaiming the kingdom. The church is at the service of the kingdom; it is meant to be a sign, a sacrament of its presence.

The kingdom is not something that we human beings fashion or build. We may sing some songs about our "building the kingdom of God," but there is no reality to be done corresponding to our words. According to the gospel imperative, we seek first the kingdom of God. We want what God wants. We desire to be totally available to God, ready to serve, eager to do God's will. Doing the will of God involves discipleship—hearing the call of Jesus and responding with the total gift of self. Doing the will of God makes the kingdom present, because we are busy about what God is busy about, and so we are where God is. Above all, as our petition teaches us, we pray for the coming of the kingdom since it is God's doing, it is God's work.

Jesus himself never gives a definition of kingdom, and we may be surprised that no one seems to question him. In the synoptic Gospels, he never claims the kingdom as his; it always is identified with the one he calls Abba. Only through parables do we find Jesus giving some description of the kingdom. Our Christian Eucharist anticipates the frequent parable allusions to the eating and drinking at the Lord's table in the kingdom. For in every Eucharist we place ourselves with Jesus in his total availability to God as he prays "not my will, but yours be done."

So what are we to say about the kingdom? How are we to make this petition our own every time we pray the Our Father? The kingdom is the inbreaking presence of God to our human world and our responsive relating to God's being with us. God continues to pour out divine life—what we name as grace—and, when human cooperation is present, then the kingdom is right at hand. Just as the disciples experienced the transfiguration of Jesus, so too the kingdom is often experienced by our touching into this transfiguration kind of moment of a deeper-down reality shining out through our ordinary world.

As we enter into the first years of the new millennium, not through the alarms of some millenarians, but rather through the gospel introduction of Jesus, we hear anew Jesus' call to conversion and repentance, his admonition of obedience and watchfulness, and his appeal to be ready and waiting. We are like members of a wedding party—joyful, expectant. But it is no bride or groom whom we serve and celebrate. It is our triune God—shining out as the redemptive presence of the Father in Jesus through the power of their Spirit of love. What do we want for ourselves and for our world? "Thy Kingdom come."

Let Us Pray

**The eyes of all look to you, Lord,
you are near to those who call.**

*Let your works praise you, Lord,
your faithful ones bless you.
Let them proclaim your glorious reign,
let them tell of your might.*

*Let them make known to all
your might and glorious reign.
Your dominion lasts for ever,
your rule for all generations!*

*The Lord is faithful in every word
and gracious in every work.
The Lord supports the fallen,
raises those bowed down.*

*The eyes of all look to you,
you give them food in due time.
You open wide your hand
to feed all living things.*

*The Lord is just in every way,
loving in every deed.
The Lord is near to those who call,
who cry out from their hearts.*

*God grants them their desires,
hears their cry and saves them.
Those who love God are kept alive;
the wicked, the Lord destroys.*

*I will sing the Lord's praise,
let all flesh bless God's Name,
holy, both now and for ever.*   Psalm 145:10-21

Discerning God's Will

Thy will be done, on earth as it is in heaven.

*T*he Our Father is the common prayer that allows Christians of whatever churches to pray together despite their differences in faith teachings and practices. One petition may be identifed as central to this prayer, especially in the light of our Christian entering into the new millennium. It is the petition that roots Jesus' prayer "that all may be one as you, Father, are in me, and I in you; I pray that they may be one in us" (Jn 17:21). The petition "Thy will be done" speaks out most clearly our renewed desire for the kind of communion among peoples, among nations, and among disciples of all the world's religions that we Christians believe is the desire of the God we are privileged to know as "Father."

This God whom we call by Jesus' love-word Abba-Father is our Creator God, the Source of all being, the One who wants us all to recognize that we are, at the deepest depths of our reality, sons and daughters through Jesus and in the Spirit and so brothers and sisters of one another. Our Christian responsibility is to put into practice our faith vision. Our vision has clarified over the centuries through our human and Christian reflective experience. But our ability to live in accord with our vision remains the test for the new age into which we have moved.

Is it ever possible for us humans to know and so do the will of God? Jesus certainly felt that he knew what God wanted and through his personal example, his teachings, and his parables tried to help us understand the direction of God for our lives. In his agony in the garden, Jesus showed that knowing the will of God and doing it does not come easy. Jesus seems to say in his prayer to Abba-Father that giving himself over to be captured, tortured, and killed does not make sense for getting the gospel preached. After all, he had been at his mission only for about three years, and while it was not a roaring success he had a number of followers. Maybe another three years, and then another, and . . . who knows? . . . the followers would be in the thousands.

Jesus wanted his mission, received from the Father, to be successful; but, above all, he wanted to do what God wanted him to do. He desired to be totally available to the One he lovingly called Abba. We are the recipients, the benefactors, of Jesus' action. Through his passion, death, and resurrection, we enjoy the consolation of his Spirit. It is that same Spirit, as St. Paul tells us, that gifts us with the rich grace of discernment. Discernment is all about making the practical life-dealing decisions, not just with prayerful prudence, but with our will attuned to the will of God our Father—our loving the way Jesus loved.

Discernment is a grace given to a lover. One who loves has a sense, a feel, for what pleases the one who is loved. A lover's instinct. To be a discerning person means that one is a free person—free of self-will, free of prejudice, free of what's expected. A discerning person can step forward for martyr-dom—not chosen by prudence but by an access of love. In a similar outpouring of love, a discerning person can choose Christ in celibate love lived in priesthood and in religious life. A discerning person enters into Christian marriage "for better, for worse, for richer, for poorer, till death do us part." A discerning person can commit to a single-life vocation. Like Jesus, a discerning person can remain available to God in what seems like some death-dealing situation, because of a faith-filled conviction that God is always the God of life. Discernment, a lover's instinct, is a special gift given to us Christians for us to know and do the will of God, just as Jesus did. Like any gift, it is never ours; it remains ever a gift—to be reverenced and esteemed and lived. That is why it is always central to the prayer that Jesus taught. "Thy will be done, on earth as it is in heaven."

Let Us Pray

**Your word is a lamp for my steps,
a light for my path, hallelujah.**

*Your word is a lamp for my steps,
a light for my path.
I have sworn firmly
to uphold your just rulings.*

*I have suffered so much,
give me the life you promise.
Receive, Lord, all that I say,
and teach me your wisdom.*

*Though danger stalks,
I will never forget your law.
Though the wicked set traps,
I will not stray from you.*

*Your laws are my heritage,
the joy of my heart for ever.
I am determined to obey
for a lasting reward.*

PSALM 119:105-112

Jubilee:
Celebrating with God

We sometimes put more into preparing for a special event than we put into the actual celebration. For example, we prepared for some years in the late 1990s to celebrate the new millennium—our efforts inspired by Pope John Paul II's *Tertio Millennio Adveniente*. Now that we have entered into the 2000s we may find ourselves forgetful of the reason for our preparations. What do we do to celebrate a biblical jubilee?

First we need to recall for ourselves the obvious. What is a biblical jubilee about? The heart of a jubilee year like 2000 is our cherishing and rejoicing in the fact that the Word was made flesh, God became man, Jesus, Son of God and Son of Mary, was born two thousand years ago. And our world has never been the same. Each of us is called anew to our following of Jesus. How well do we know him? Despite the frequency with which we are exposed to the acronym WWJD, do we feel confident in acting out our response to the question "What would Jesus do?" The very title we proudly bear—Christian—suggests that others can expect to see in us a face of Christ, his action, his love, and his forgiveness. Perhaps, first of all, any jubilee celebration reminds us that we are always renewing our effort to foster our friendship with Christ.

looking at the church year

81

Prisms for a Christ-Life

As we search out the ways helpful to us for growing in our knowledge and love of Jesus (for example, spiritual reading, Bible study, prayer, Eucharist, volunteer service projects), we may find that Jesus' reference to the jubilee text in Isaiah 61 as he proclaims his own mission in Luke 4:18-19 can become our entrance into a way of celebration:

The spirit of the Lord is upon me; therefore he has anointed me. He has sent me to bring glad tidings to the poor, to proclaim liberty to captives, recovery of sight to the blind, and release to prisoners, to announce a year of favor from the Lord.

The context for such a mission for Jesus and so for us is "to be anointed," "to be sent." The biblical concept of jubilee involves, above all, a call from God. As we make attempts to find ways that we can celebrate, more than rushing to take on pious devotions or volunteer ministries, we need to listen to the call of God in our life. A little more reflection time—listening time—is a pervading essential of a jubilee. Jubilee and Sabbath are intimately connected since jubilee is God's expansion of the Sabbath rest. But rest in relation to God is not defined as inactivity; rather, Sabbath centers us on taking time for our relationship with God, for enhancing that relationship. In a jubilee time we respond to God's initiative in our way of celebrating rather than assume the initiative ourselves. Our behavior, then, would be like Jesus'—who describes himself as sent. For Jesus, the initiative is always God's. Our celebrating jubilee begins with our taking the time to be a listener, our being available to God's initiative, our making the effort to enhance our relationship with God.

Just as jubilee is related to Sabbath, so jubilee is also related to Sunday, the day of Jesus' resurrection. Jubilee celebrates a new beginning: drawing on new reserves of resources (for those who feel empty and poor), seeking new visions (for those who are blind or in the dark), enjoying new freedom (for those who suffer from feeling limited and bound). The jubilee ideal for the Israelite people was spelled out in such concrete actions as returning land to original settlers, setting free the slave or servant, and letting the land lie fallow. Every action looked to a newness of life, a renewed beginning. Jesus assumed this dimension of the jubilee ideal as his mission and gave it divine meaning in his resurrection. We, the followers of Jesus and the recipients of his Spirit, continue to follow his example as we celebrate jubilee: we listen to God, we follow God's lead, we imitate Jesus, we act like Christians. Maybe a jubilee celebration is a time for us to confound G.K. Chesterton's witty and yet poignant judgment: "The Christian ideal has not been tried and found wanting. It has been found difficult; and left untried." Our celebration means that we determine to act like Christians, day in day out, all year long. The world around us certainly would be different. We would know a jubilee.

Let Us Pray

How good to sing God praise!
How lovely the sound!

I will never stop thanking God,
with constant words of praise.
My soul will boast of God;
the poor will hear me and be glad.

Join me in praising the Lord,
together tell of God's name.
I asked and the Lord responded,
freed me from all my fears.

Turn to God, be bright with joy;
you shall never be let down.
I begged and God heard,
took my burdens from me.

God's angel defends the faithful,
guards them on every side.
Drink in the richness of God,
enjoy the strength of the Lord.

PSALM 34:2-9

Holy Celebration

*T*he biblical notion of jubilee implies celebration. The Advent and Christmas seasons provide an opportune moment for us to consider what it is that we celebrate.

Celebration often means bringing people together, sometimes those dearest to us, and at other times the "crowd" that comes together only for special occasions. Celebration can include elegant banquets or simple finger food. It may suggest a refined cocktail party or a noisy beer-keg-and-pretzels get-together. Celebration can imply long-term planning or it may be a spur-of-the-moment, spontaneous occasion. We celebrate beginnings, like newborn babies and the wedding day; we celebrate completions, like school graduations and retirements. We observe national patriotic days, and we take time for religious festivals.

But, for all the aspects of a biblical jubilee year—forgiveness, justice, reconciliation—what is it that we most celebrate? The biblical notion of jubilee celebrates, above all, our being God's people and our living like God's sons and daughters. This planet called Earth is "home" for us because it is God's home. Our space-age view of our planet Earth has brought home to us how much we all are "stewards," not owners, of God's gift to us.

What is striking is how our jubilee celebrations enter us into the Gospel's Prodigal Son parable. Whether we more identify with one who hopes to see life as only an arena of personal delights and squanderings or whether we more identify with the other, who defines life as a kind of slavery with weighty obligations and grim duties, we realize how much we need a jubilee understanding of life. Both sons, in Jesus' famous parable, understand neither the father who helped bring them into life nor the life which this father wants to share with them. The first son in his self-centered celebrating misses the point of celebration. The second son in his self-defined servitude also misses the idea of celebration. Just as the father in the parable goes out of the way to meet each son, so God continues to break into our life to call us to a reality of biblical jubilee.

Advent is our jubilee celebration of our longing and desire to dwell in the house of the Lord all the days of our life. Christmas is our jubilee celebration of God's desire and longing to come and play forever among the children of Earth. Advent and Christmas are at the center of our understanding of jubilee because both seasons emphasize the heart of all our reasons to celebrate: God calls us sons and daughters, and we know the redemptive salvation that Jesus brought, of living in God's home all the days of our life.

Let Us Pray

Lord our God, the whole world tells the greatness of your name.

Lord our God,
the whole world tells
the greatness of your name.
Your glory reaches
beyond the stars.

Even the babble of infants
declares your strength,
your power to halt
the enemy and avenger.

I see your handiwork
in the heavens:
The moon and the stars
you set in place.

What is humankind
that you remember them,
the human race
that you care for them?

You treat them like gods,
dressing them in glory and splendor.
You give them charge of the earth,
laying all at their feet:

cattle and sheep,
wild beasts,
birds of the sky,
fish of the sea,
every swimming creature.

Lord our God,
the whole world tells
the greatness of your name.

PSALM 8

Keeping Holy the Sabbath

Sabbath has always been identified with the seventh day—the day of the Lord's rest after the six days' work of creation as depicted in chapter one of the Book of Genesis. The Christian tradition reidentified the Lord's day with the resurrection victory of Jesus, bringing to fullness the work of redemption.

The idea of refraining from work has often received greater attention even though the church has always identified "making holy" the Lord's day—Sunday—by the twofold obligation of celebrating the Eucharist and doing no *servile* work. Of course, there has been a lot of moral casuistry applied to the meaning of servile work, so much, perhaps, that the focus on God slipped because of the overwhelming emphasis on human activity—what was right, what was wrong, how long or how drudging could the work be, and so on. We are always being called to move beyond the casuistry and to recapture the spirit of the Sabbath.

Sabbath means, above all, a chosen awareness of spending time with God. If we are to spend time with God, then we have to take time for ourselves—not just time filled up with more "doing," even with passive sporting events or active participations in games, but time which we describe so well today in terms of just "being." Sabbath is meant to be a deeply humane time because then God can become more active in us. Sabbath points to the movement of the oft-quoted expression of St. Irenaeus: "God's glory is the human being come fully alive, and seeing God is what human life is."

Eucharist belongs to the Christian Sunday observance because we celebrate God's glory shining out in the victorious risen Jesus, the firstborn of the new creation. But what else belongs to our Sabbath observance? What enhances our relationship with God? In other words, how do we devote time to making ourselves more humane—loving, compassionate, wise, generous, available, sharing—so that God's glory does shine out now through us? When we truly observe the Sabbath, we are more and more like the sacraments of God that our Christian vocation calls us to be.

Another viewpoint. We can consider our idea of vacation time. Vacation, being personal rest time, shares in the Sabbath notion. We sometimes refer to spiritual retreats as "vacations with God." Retreats, of course, take their focus from considering our relation with God. But would we be acting more Christian if we viewed ordinary vacation time through a prism similar to our Sunday observance? Vacation time does not need to be spent "religiously," performing devotional prayers and acts. But would it not be appropriate for us Christians to spend our recuperative and relaxing time with a more spiritual focus? Vacation means a time of "emptying out" (of mental cobwebs and secular preoccupations) and a "leaving space" (for attention to an ever present and loving God) in the ordinariness of our life.

"Keep holy the Sabbath day," then, should draw our attention not to what is to be avoided, but to what enhances our relationship with God, with ourselves, with our neighbor, and with our world. Those relationships are meant to be observed together, as a whole, when we speak of "keeping holy." Keeping holy deals with all our relationships viewed in the light of God and Jesus Christ. When we keep holy, we move with the Spirit. We let ourselves be moved by the Spirit—with all those with whom we converse, in all things we do.

Jubilee, Sabbath, and our secular vacation all find their meaning in the one reality of celebrating God in our life. Jubilees, Sabbaths, and vacations come to us not by some kind of law or right, but by gift—the gift of God. These time periods remind us to take stock and enjoy the God-with-us now so that we take from these "moments" the realized promise and consolation of our lifetime with God forever.

Let Us Pray

The sky tells the glory of God.

The sky tells the glory of God,
tells the genius of God's work.
Day carries the news to day,
night brings the message to night,

without a word, without a sound,
without a voice being heard,
yet their message fills the world,
their news reaches its rim.

There God has pitched a tent
for the sun to rest and rise renewed
like a bridegroom rising from bed,
an athlete eager to run the race.

It springs from the edge of the earth,
runs a course across the sky
to win the race at heaven's end.
Nothing on earth escapes its heat.

PSALM 19:2-7

Celebrating Christmas

*W*henever we celebrate the feast of Christmas, we come face-to-face with our ways of imaging and understanding God. Drawing close to a baby in a manger does not seem difficult for young or old, for shepherds or theologians. Yet the implications of such an imaging need to be appropriated anew by people in every age and culture.

The Christmas tableau challenges our way of evaluating ourselves, our relationships with others, and our own response to God. People of our time, we find it natural to stress our personal gifts and talents; we look to our strength in self-image and our self-reliance in thought and action. And, yes, we are made aware of a lot of proper healthy correctives given to us today by the psychological sciences. We are encouraged to pull our own strings, to be confrontal and even aggressive in pursuing our goals. Yet the angels' Gloria trumpeted above a stable reminds us that human dignity and personal choice are not values without restrictions or limits. Today our relationship with God centers often on gender-imaging, but with the result that something like "the force be with you" expresses the compromise of a god-without-a-face.

In the midst of some overly serious abstract arguments and of our age's all-too-limiting focus on personal experience comes a human baby named Jesus, whose mother is Mary. Each time we place ourselves in wonder before this crèche, we are enabled to glimpse some of the deepest realities about divine and human life.

Jesus comes to us as poor and humble. He is poor, not only because like any baby he is totally dependent for food and shelter on others, but also because he incarnates God's chosen way of relating to us. Jesus shows us a God who truly needs us, who waits upon our response, who suffers our indifference as well as our petty insistences on making gods more to our own liking. Jesus brings home to us that God is not a mighty one who delights in hurling lightning bolts or an impassive one seated on a cloud and forever lost in contemplation. We rejoice in being led to a God who has chosen to make himself so needy that our efforts can fill what is still lacking in the redemptive act and that our prayers and our actions have their contribution to make in building up the community of the city of God.

In fact, in recognizing such a God, we know that being poor is not a curse but a grace that makes us more like God. When we recognize our neediness as a fact in our relation to others and to God, then our poverty is truly becoming our graced choice. We are becoming like Jesus; divinity becomes us.

Again like any poor person, the Son of Mary and the carpenter must labor for the necessities of life. He will say that everything he has is gift given by the one he knows as Abba, but at the same time, because this God is one who works, Jesus matter-of-factly professes "I work." And from the very beginning Jesus calls others to labor with him—so reminiscent of that creation account of God asking the first humans to work in bringing the garden to a greater fruitfulness. Jesus again brings home to all of us that God is the first of collaborators. If we want to grow more in the divine life, our direction is clear. To work with others is the dynamic of Christian living—in families, in workplaces, in parishes and religious communities, in ecumenical endeavors, in civil society.

To celebrate Christmas is not to seek escape into magical stars and angels singing and plum puddings and once-a-year friendly greetings. We Christians worship a God who chooses to be poor like us so that we may make a similar choice and thus realize a richness which can only be God's gift. We Christians step forward to take on the responsibility of collaboration with God for the coming of the kingdom; like our God, we catch sight of our real selves not in doing our good works for others, but always in acting with others. God so loved the world

Prisms for a Christ-Life

. . . and in our so living and in our so working we make real our love for God, ourselves, our neighbor, and our world.

Let Us Pray

The Lord is my saving light; whom should I fear?

One thing I ask the Lord,
one thing I seek:
to live in the house of God
every day of my life,
caught up in God's beauty,
at prayer in his temple.

The Lord will hide me there,
hide my life from attack:
a sheltering tent above me,
a firm rock below.

I am now beyond reach
of those who besiege me.
In his temple I will offer
a joyful sacrifice,
I will play and sing to God.

PSALM 27:4-6

Darkness and Light

Recently in the city of St. Louis, Missouri, at the end of a rainy day the clouds on the western horizon broke just enough to let the rays of a setting sun produce a brilliant and full rainbow. The rainbow lasted so long, the colors were so distinct, that local TV and newspaper journalists could not resist expressing their marvel. I was struck once again at how we humans are captivated by the phenomenon of light.

If we want to celebrate a civic or social event, we light up the darkness of night with a dazzling array of fireworks. The beauty of a modern city is often measured by the lighting, sometimes hard and defining, at other times soft and mellow, which enhances its major buildings and monuments. The wonder of Christmas displays, whether secular ones in store windows or religious ones in church and home, is generated by the twinkling of myriads of starlike light bulbs. We find a fascination with light, even if we are fortunate enough to live in a take-it-for-granted electric light world.

Perhaps our fascination with light remains because we feel so easily oppressed by earth's darkness. In a winter season we endure with some dismay the shortness of daylight hours bracketed by both late-morning and early-afternoon darkness. In season and out, we suffer the dark burden of sickness and death among family and friends. Exposed to media coverage, we feel weighed down by the dark oppression of people's hatred, prejudice, torturing, and killing of one another, whether it be in Bosnia or Rwanda or our own city.

During the months of November and December, church tradition emphasizes two aspects of light shining into the darkness of human experience. The sure coming of the reign of God shines out in the month of November, as we approach the end of Ordinary Time, through three distinctive feasts—All Saints, All Souls, and Christ the King. All Souls, the commemoration of all the faithful departed, might seem at first sight to be a "dark" feast that sets the tone for this month of our remembering the dead. But the companion feastdays of All Saints and All Souls become twin lights beckoning all of us in the church on earth to struggle on in our graced efforts to let God's reign shine forth here and now. The feast of Christ the King suggests searchlight beams striding across nighttime clouds and presenting a preview glimpse of the incarnate Son's eschatological joy as the Father brings "all things in the heavens and on earth into one under Christ's headship" (Ep 1:10). Our faith is stirred to shine through any present darkness: "We believe in the life of the world to come." In the rainbow light of these feasts, we are led again to profess in word and in action the sureness of our faith's goal.

Then we turn from the darkness that seems to obscure human life's purpose and direction to a darkness in which not despair and death but the beginnings of hope and life are hidden. December holds the dark tradition of centuries-long human searching and hoping portrayed in the season of Advent, which breaks forth into the pure shining beam over Jesus' birth, the celebration of the nativity of our Lord. We proclaim that "a light has shone in our darkness." Celebrating Christmas we do not just remember a past event, but we enter anew into our own Christian responsibility to "shine like the stars in the sky while holding fast to the word of life" (Ph 2:15-16).

Let Us Pray

**Sing and bless God's name,
tell God's triumph day to day.**

*A new song for the Lord!
Sing it and bless God's name,
everyone, everywhere!
Tell the whole world
God's triumph day to day,
God's glory, God's wonder.*

*A noble God deserving praise,
the dread of other gods,
the puny gods of pagans;
for our God made the heavens —
the Lord of majestic light
who fills the temple with beauty.*

*Proclaim the Lord, you nations,
praise the glory of God's power,
praise the glory of God's name!
Bring gifts to the temple,
bow down, all the earth,
tremble in God's holy presence.*

*Tell the nations, "The Lord rules!"
As the firm earth is not swayed,
nothing can sway God's judgment.
Let the heaven and earth be glad,
the sea and sea creature roar,
the field and its beasts exult.*

*Then let the trees of the forest sing
before the coming of the Lord,
who comes to judge the nations,
to set the earth aright,
restoring the world to order.* PSALM 96

Prisms for a Christ-Life

Being Human

For those who take their Christian calendar for granted, the celebration of Christmas day seems more an ordinary part of the secular year than the extraordinary event it is. In the case of the business retailer, the days leading up to Christmas become the watershed for a profitable sales year. For those in school the Christmas season marks the end of a semester, perhaps a graduation, or at least a holiday time. There are large parts of Muslim, Jewish, Buddhist, and Hindu worlds where Christmas remains a Western cultural "playtime" invention. And what is Christmas really for us?

Christmas celebrates an almost unbelievable reality: God being born as a human being, as a rather ordinary helpless baby. As usual with the arrival of a baby, Christmas represents joy, and with the magical ingredients of angels singing, shepherds watching, and Magi adoring we seem to hold Life with a gentle and light touch. Yet we cannot ignore the dark side of Christmas and the various struggles present within its story, such as the massacre of the innocent babies and the refugee reality of this young family in Egypt. One continuing struggle we all enter into as Christians is in believing that God loves this tangled human world so much. Another contemporary area of conflict for us lies in the chosen limitations which God takes on in being human, for example, in being male, not female, in being Jewish, not Irish, Polish, or Japanese, in being an uneducated, itinerant preacher, not a priest, a lawyer, or a successful financier. Certain things will be remembered about Jesus — this

God-man—ways of speaking, the kinds of stories he told, his program for what it means to be blessed. All of this sets up the potential for more conflict and misunderstanding from this Middle Eastern way of approaching life so different from our own.

Perhaps in our time we need to enter into Christmas more from God's point of view of our human world rather than fixating on our own conflictual struggles. Today it seems that causes and movements, allegiances and prejudices, tend to make us small, mean, and even vindictive. Christmas takes on new importance for us Christians when the reality we celebrate allows us to identify with God in smallness and in the mean things of this world. We enter a little more lightly and gently into the conflict of limitations which God so eagerly took on in Jesus—the one we call our Vindicator. God desires to minister to a world out of love even though some forms and expressions of love always seem to be the source of so much misunderstanding and conflict.

Always the energy of love which seeks union and draws forth imitation enhances at the same time the differentiation of the ones in love. Teilhard de Chardin's evolution axiom, "Union differentiates," restates more secularly the Pauline concept of the glory of differences in hands and feet and eye within the Body of Christ—all united in the love of Christ in God.

Our contemporary struggle with our own human sexuality in relating to our Christian God needs to find softer focus within the light of Christmas. Maybe there is a kind of divine humor in speaking and relating to God in masculine and feminine imagery. After all, if sexuality makes no sense in referring to our trinitarian God's life, at least the origins of our own human sexuality—limiting as it is in its male and female forms—stem from our creator God of love. And so in accentuating our masculine and feminine realities we reflect back some kind of reality within God's life. Jesus only makes concrete in his very person the struggle of our human love of God—both towards himself and to the God he calls Abba, Father.

May the God enfleshed for us, celebrated anew each Christmas season, help us touch issues and challenges of our times lightly, gently, and with grace.

Let Us Pray

**The Lord, my God, has dressed me
in robes of justice and victory.**

*I sing out with joy to the Lord,
all that I am delights in God,
for the Lord has dressed me
in robes of justice and victory,
like a groom wearing a garland
or a bride arrayed in jewels.*

*As earth causes seed to sprout,
and gardens make plants grow,
so justice and praise spring from God
for all the nations to see.*

*For Zion's sake I speak out,
for Jerusalem I do not rest,
till her victory shines like the sun,
blazes out like a torch.*

*The world will see your deliverance,
all kings witness your glory.
They will know you by a new name
which the Lord will give you.
Your walls and towers will shine forth,
a royal crown in God's hand.*

*They will no longer call you Forsaken,
nor your land Barren.
Beloved will be your name,
and your land will be called Married.
For the Lord delights in you,
and your fields will be fertile.*

*As a young man marries a wife,
your Builder will marry you.
As a groom delights in his bride,
the Lord will honor you.*

ISAIAH 61:10-62:5

The Human Level

*A*ll of us have to be born and have to die. These "have to's" sound like some activity we must do, when both are rather something that happens to us. "Being born" and "being dying" are the leveling events that bookend all human life. What fills the space in between seems to spell out nothing but all the hills and valleys, rolling vineyards and desert wastelands, that represent the inequalities of human living.

Some people are born into wealth, and they will never know want. Others are only fortunate enough at birth to have a mother healthy enough to give them mother's milk, but they will go through life malnourished and disease-prone. Some are born highly gifted and fail ever to develop their talents. Others struggle through life with a minimum of human endowments, but successfully act with a perennial zest. Some seem to sail through life's events as though they were on a tranquil sea. Others seem to be wracked by storms and earthquakes as part of life's context. Some will spend their life in steel and glass skyscrapers, and others will know only the simplest of grass or plywood huts. Some will travel the world; others will know only their village. Except for "being born" and "being dying," we human beings seem to spend lifetimes of greatly unequal value. There seems to be no level playing field for all people to encounter each other on.

God engages the inequalities of human life in the incarnation and birth of his Son. In the familiar hymn quoted in St. Paul's letter to the Philippians, our attitude must be "that of

Christ: "Though he was in the form of God, he did not deem equality with God something to be grasped at. Rather, he emptied himself and took the form of a slave, being born in the likeness of men. He was known to be of human estate, and it was thus that he humbled himself, obediently accepting even death, death on a cross" (Ph 2: 5-9).

Paul reflects that God takes on a true inequality. In becoming human, Christ goes from the fullness of divinity to the emptiness of humanity. Theologically, humanity is empty because everything that each of us has is gift, as Jesus reminds us in saying that all his words and his works are not his, but come from the Father. So in faith we know an inequality that is real between God and the human. But, then, in God's becoming human in Jesus, we come to know God's definitive action in breaking down all the appearances of inequality that divide us humans.

Jesus entered into the leveling experience of all humans by "being born" and by "being dying." Through all the in-between time, he lived his life as an example and taught by word and parable that the leveling process permeated the whole of human living. In St. Luke's Gospel, Jesus gives his sermon, not on the mount as in St. Matthew's, but on the level plain when he invites us to live a life of the beatitudes. While friendly with rich and poor alike, with learned and unlearned, Jesus seems to violate our sense of leveling by his identifying with the poor, with servants and slaves, with the marginalized. He reaches out to them in his care; he tells stories about them for our instruction. Jesus asks us to be like him—one who serves. In the Last Supper washing of the feet, Jesus stresses that he has given us an example.

Jesus transfigures the language and meaning of slavery, service, and ministry.

All these words now describe valued human interaction from a divine perspective. We all are meant to be helpers—in Scripture, sometimes called slaves, sometimes servants, sometimes ministers—to one another in life. Helpers and those being helped are on the same level. One is not superior as a human being in either being the helper or minister or being the one being helped or ministered to. Jesus gave us an unforgettable image by answering "Who is my neighbor?" with the parable of the Good Samaritan. The second half of the one commandment stresses that we love our neighbor as ourselves. Our love goes out to whomever, persons always on a level no different from ourselves. We neither reach down in helping nor reach up; we only reach across. By entering into our human level, God broke through all the specious levels that seem to divide humankind. By our entering into the divine experience of Jesus, we see and act as sons and daughters of a heavenly Father.

Every Christmas we challenge ourselves anew about the Christian leveling of human life. By our faith we live life on the same level—the level has been forever divinely clarified because of the birth of Jesus.

Let Us Pray

Where charity and love are found, there is God.

Our God is good, give thanks!
God's love is for ever!
Our God of gods, give thanks!
God's love is for ever!
Our Lord of lords, give thanks!
God's love is for ever!

Alone the maker of worlds!
God's love is for ever!
Architect for the skies!
God's love is for ever!
Spread land on the sea!
God's love is for ever!

Set the great lights above!
God's love is for ever!
The sun to rule the day!
God's love is for ever!
The moon and stars, the night!
God's love is for ever!   PSALM 136:1-9

Prisms for a Christ-Life

Justice and Reconciliation

*O*ne of the striking aspects of John Paul II's encyclicals, apostolic exhortations, and papal audience presentations has been their focus on a reconciling or unifying theme. *Orientale lumen* clearly is a call for even greater efforts in seeking a reconciliation between the Orthodox churches and the Latin-rite Roman church and the Eastern rites in communion with Rome. *Ut unum sint* looks to a time of unity for all Christian churches, founded on the reconciling role of the bishop of Rome. Justice for past wrongs is not a precondition, only forgiveness.

Where liberation theology, in particular, helped the Christian community to see more clearly the necessary relationship of our baptismal faith and justice, the movement for human rights in all of its ramifications now appears to be entering a new depth. In the Christian dispensation, reconciliation is the heart of divine justice. God's just judgment in the face of human evil and sin takes shape in the reconciling life, death, and resurrection of Jesus. Only through Christian revelation do we hear that justice finds its center in reconciliation. That is why St. Paul could exuberantly proclaim that we as ministers of Christ truly are ambassadors of reconciliation.

Since the 1971 synod's document on "Justice in the World," there has been a certain amount of turmoil in the church, especially in Latin America, over the shape and direction of justice efforts. Religious life communities wholeheartedly took up the challenge of faith and its relation to justice in their chapters of renewal and in their production of mission documents. Mixed signals of encouragement and disapproval came forth from Roman dicasteries, from national episcopal conferences, and sometimes even from a divisive ferment within a religious congregation itself. For those church congregations and religious life groups which had grown all too comfortable with a Western world middle- and upper-class lifestyle, living a faith that does justice (and does not escape into a charity-alone approach) is to heed the call to conversion found at the start of each of the Gospels. Necessary as this call is for every age, it took on a crucial importance in the post-World War II development of nations, particularly between northern and southern hemispheres. But as our past quarter-century experience has brought home, the human sense of justice runs independently of Christian faith, and, for lay Catholics as well as for women and men religious, justice efforts can break off from faith roots. Then the result appears as a burnout activism, deeper divisiveness, and greater injustice.

The call coming to us as we enter into the new millennium is not a reversal of our Christian efforts to work for a world in which there are more just relationships among all peoples. The call is for us to keep our attention fixed on the heart of all justice efforts which Christians exercise. An emphasis on righteousness only has led in our experience to conflict and further injustice. Just relations in human living are doomed to frustration and failure without a centering in forgiveness and reconciliation. If we ultimately are not about a ministry of reconciliation in our justice efforts, we are not about a Christian ministry. Perhaps that is why each year we need to hear anew voices from heaven singing out "peace and goodwill" as we welcome God's own Ambassador of reconciliation.

Let Us Pray

**I sing to you, my God,
and live the truth I sing.**

*I sing to you, O Lord,
sing your justice and love,
and live the truth I sing.
When will you come to me?*

*I show my royal household
how to lead a perfect life.
I shun what is devious
and hate deceit—
it can never touch me.*

*The wicked dare not approach me,
for I am no friend to evil.
I silence those who gossip,
I detest their vanity and pride.*

*I look for loyal people
to share my palace.
Those who live honest lives
will serve me.*

*I cannot bear scoundrels and liars,
they are not welcome in my house.
My daily work
is to rid the land of evil
and cleanse the City of God.*

PSALM 101

Seeking New Life

The desire for new life, new ideas, new expressions, new insights permeates the everyday existence of us all. Modern-day advertising and the consumer economy of first-world countries continuously search out the ways to sell products, not in terms of real needs, but in terms of induced needs for something new. Consumerism builds upon the human desire for the new, while at the same time offsetting the equally strong human tendency to remain comfortably entrenched in the familiar.

The church seasons of Lent and Easter confront us all with our desires for the new and with our equally strong tendency to remain firmly entrenched where we are. The dialogue between Nicodemus and Jesus in the third chapter of St. John's Gospel captures well the continuing exchange between the Christian and God, clearly focused during these church seasons. Approaching God out of a certain darkness in our lives, we seek new life and new growth, a new understanding of our faith, or a new sense of relationship with God and with neighbor. But when God starts indicating a dying to some familiar life patterns, when God starts pointing the way to "being born anew," we are tempted to laugh it off, to claim we are "too old" to need that kind of change. Why not a little "renewal," perhaps a little "restoration," or maybe even an attempt to "recapture" past devotion or past grace (charism)? Any of these words seem to allow us to keep some measure of control, to retain something of the old and familiar, and yet to pray and give God a place.

Rebirth—to be born anew—remains the challenge of Lent and Easter. Rebirth means the dying and rising—the pattern of the paschal mystery—which we Christians celebrate in the daily Eucharist. More clearly in these Lenten and Easter seasons we come face-to-face with the most traditional faith concept—that it is the Spirit who brings to birth and who gives life, in our continuing personal growth in our life-in-Christ, in the life of our religious congregations, and in the life of our church both local and larger.

May the joy with which the risen Jesus consoles us now become more richly our experience of new life.

Let Us Pray

**God rescues me from death,
steadying my feet.**

*I am filled with love,
for the Lord hears me;
the Lord bends to my voice
whenever I call.*

*Death had me in its grip,
the grave's trap was set,
grief held me fast.
I cried out for God,
"Please, Lord, rescue me!"*

*Kind and faithful is the Lord,
gentle is our God.
The Lord shelters the poor,
raises me from the dust.
Rest once more, my heart,
for you know the Lord's love.*

*God rescues me from death,
wiping my tears,
steadying my feet.
I walk with the Lord
in this land of the living.* PSALM 116:1-9

Making a Difference

*P*ierre Teilhard de Chardin in *The Divine Milieu* observes that the larger half of our lives is made up of what happens to us. His observation comes home to us each year as we celebrate the great high holy days of Christianity—Holy Thursday, Good Friday, Holy Saturday, and Easter Sunday. Paradoxically Jesus accomplishes the work of redemption, his life's purpose, in what happens to him in his suffering, death, and resurrection. We enter into this paradox by our celebration of these days. We cannot change history, we cannot undo what has happened. Our celebration allows us in our own time to enter into what happened to Jesus and to be with him, to stand alongside, to feel compassion—as helplessly as we listen to someone tell of being tortured by a totalitarian regime or as we sit at the bedside of a dying loved one. No activity of ours changes the event; compassionate presence is the difficult but precious gift we can give. Of course, it is also our privilege to share in someone's joy and happiness, as we do when we celebrate the resurrection victory of Jesus.

Despite the fact that so many of us are spectator-sports people, whether in the stadium or in front of the TV set, we are not comfortable being spectators of an evil we cannot eliminate and sometimes even of a happiness which little touches our lives. We may find other people's parties empty of fun for ourselves, and we may dread visiting a neighbor in the hospital. We would rather not drive through derelict inner-city neighborhoods, we would brush past the homeless person sleeping over heating grates in our downtowns, or we would switch TV channels if the images of starving Sudanese children with distended stomachs are too graphic. The problems seem too large for our efforts to make a difference. Our activity and our emotions seem frozen. Even though we are members of the Body of Christ, we often choose not to see and not to hear.

When hostages return exuberantly to waiting families, when a comatose girl revives to the joy of her parents, when government agencies extend unemployment benefits for those hurting in a recession economy, how often do we feel a thrill and utter a prayer of thanks to God? Too often we keep ourselves emotionally distant even from the *joys* of others around us, probably because they just "happen" and leave us personally unaffected. St. Paul could state, in the analogy of our human bodies, that if one member suffers all the members suffer with it; if one member is honored, all the members share its joy.

The Easter events challenge us always in what we do and in what happens to us. If God is truly the God of our life, then we find the opportunity of meeting God both in what we set out to do and in what happens to us. Jesus' crucifixion confronts the activist in each of us to question our judgment about our most valued "work." All of our dyings become not the entropy of exhaustive waste, but graced moments of freedom to embrace another givenness of life from our God of life.

When St. Paul challenged death—"Where is your sting?"—he did not close his eyes to the evils and losses which all the forms of dying represent. He trumpeted the Easter message that the Christ-redemption event changes not only our attitude but also our ability to value the whole of our life—its successes and accomplishments, its apparent waste matter of sin and failure. As Gospel models, Mary Magdalene (who may have confused sex and love) and Peter (who has grabbed for success and lied for survival) are the first among the evangelizers of this new creation event.

Pope John Paul's appeal for a new evangelization takes form in us by our renewed attempt to integrate the active and passive aspects of our daily life. By living faith-lives as "other Christs" we make a difference in what we do and in what we suffer. The call to a new evangelization invites us to explore further the struggles of justice and poverty and human living both at our doorstep and in our larger world. Making a difference often seems like planting seeds and having to wait for things to happen. Easter faith stirs us up in hope, moves us out in action, and integrates us in a compassionate patience.

May the risen Lord embrace us anew with the grace of his passion for life.

Let Us Pray

**God will bless all believers,
the small and the great, hallelujah.**

*Not to us, Lord, not to us,
but to your name give glory,
because of your love,
because of your truth.*

*Why do the nations say,
"Where is their God?"
Our God is in the heavens
and answers to no one.*

*Their gods are crafted by hand,
mere silver and gold,
with mouths that are mute
and eyes that are blind,
with ears that are deaf
and noses that cannot smell.*

*Their hands cannot feel,
their feet cannot walk,
their throats are silent.
Their makers, their worshipers
will be just like them.*

Let Israel trust God,
their help and shield.
Let the house of Aaron trust God,
their help and shield.
Let all believers trust God,
their help and shield.

The Lord has remembered us
and will bless us,
will bless the house of Israel,
will bless the house of Aaron.
God will bless all believers,
the small and the great.

May God bless you more and more,
bless all your children.
May you truly be blessed
by the maker of heaven and earth.

To the Lord belong the heavens,
to us the earth below!
The dead sing no Hallelujah,
nor do those in the silent ground.
But we will bless you, Lord,
now and for ever.

Hallelujah!

PSALM 115

Disappointments and Resurrection

We do not necessarily compliment ourselves when we compare ourselves to the first disciples of Jesus. For example, the two disciples on their way to Emmaus do not symbolize either gospel people (evangelizers) or apostolic people (on a mission). In a way, of course, they are pilgrim people, journeying, although they are running away from Jerusalem, where their lives are meant to be centered. They know a lot about Jesus—enough to keep talking about him at least between themselves or privately with an amiable stranger. Yet what stands out in their telling of the Jesus story is their own disappointment.

Disappointment may be the common cross that afflicts us followers of Jesus all the more because we like to describe ourselves as Alleluia people. These two disciples symbolize disappointment immediately after Jesus' passion. During the active ministry of Jesus, a rich man with much fervor wanted to lead a holy life, but walked away from Jesus—disappointed with his kind of "Beatitude" challenge. Other disciples caused Jesus such pain by their leaving that he asked Peter and the others identified as the Twelve, "Will you leave me too?" People had left chagrined by all this foolish talk about Jesus being the food and drink of their lives. They were unwilling to live with promise in such incarnate guise.

Disappointment can certainly be a difficult cross to bear for us Christ-followers. For us present-day disciples of the one who has overcome death, it somehow seems "not right" to have to continue to face defeat, failure, and betrayal, especially from

111

agents that speak or act in Christ's name. How can we not be disappointed when the Vatican at one time was the sole agency among all the world's states which recognized a repressive government in Haiti? How legitimate the disappointment is when we face the problem of certain clerics or religious who betrayed a trust by their sexual abuse of a child! How disappointing for us as a community is the high percentage of failed marriages, often within our own families—marriages celebrated with all the beauty and solemn commitment of the wedding Mass! Are we ever disappointed with ourselves—after years of striving to be Little Flowers—at still feeling more like the scrubby weeds found along abandoned railroad tracks?

Disappointments come in all sizes—some so big that they seem insurmountable, but others so small and daily that we suffer them as the necessary "colds and flu" of our spiritual life. Disappointments come at all stages of life development. Young and old and all the in-betweens face unrealized or shattered dreams, an if-only sense of things left undone, feelings of abandonment by loved ones.

Where does the event of Christ's resurrection touch most directly the practical living of our lives? I would suggest that we need to look towards our experience of disappointments. We test quickly the firmness of our faith in the resurrection by our lived response to disappointment. Among us followers who want to distance ourselves from this hierarchical church or to walk away from a disheartened priesthood or to dismiss a seemingly anachronistic religious life or to reject a cumbersome parish structure, we find an identity with the two disciples on their way to Emmaus. The question we face is whether we will take the time from all our talk or activity to listen to and recognize the call to believe what is central to our faith: Jesus is risen, and our response to disappointment need never be a time without grace, an experience without new life. The Easter event translates into our creedal "I believe in the resurrection of the dead." But the daily disappointments that make us die by inches are where we all need to let our resurrection faith have its effect. As with the two disciples on that first Easter evening, it is in our hurrying back into a disappointing Jerusalem—with our faith in the risen Lord—that we truly act as evangelizers and people on mission.

Let Us Pray

**This is the day the Lord has made,
let us rejoice and be glad.**

*I was pushed to falling,
but the Lord gave me help.
My strength, my song is the Lord,
who has become my savior.*

*Glad songs of victory sound
within the tents of the just.
With right hand raised high,
the Lord strikes with force.*

*I shall not die but live
to tell the Lord's great deeds.
The Lord punished me severely,
but did not let me die.*

*Open the gates of justice,
let me praise God within them.
This is the Lord's own gate,
only the just will enter.
I thank you for you answered me,
and you became my savior.*

*The stone the builders rejected
has become the cornerstone.
This is the work of the Lord,
how wonderful in our eyes.*

*This is the day the Lord made,
let us rejoice and be glad.
Lord, give us the victory!
Lord, grant us success!
Blest is the one who comes,
who comes in the name of the Lord.*

Prisms for a Christ-Life

We bless you from the Lord's house.
The Lord God is our light:
adorn the altar with branches.

I will thank you, my God,
I will praise you highly.
Give thanks, the Lord is good,
God's love is for ever!

PSALM 118:13-29

Ordinary Year

The word ordinary seems to imply the bland, the unexciting, the run-of-the-mill, the everyday. In fact, for many of us even the liturgical year of the church suffers from being divided into two parts: the Seasons and Ordinary Time. Although liturgy properly speaks of our celebrations, we tend to find it hard to celebrate what is called ordinary.

Perhaps the very distinction which the church highlights in so dividing the liturgical year calls us to a deeper reflection upon our understanding of the ordinary.

God creates the ordinary . . . and calls it good. It is true: the ordinary is the very substance of our world. While being itself God's creation, the ordinary is also the substance with which God works. We, by being ordinary, can be touched and molded and transfigured by God.

Often we try to escape from being ordinary, and in the process we shut ourselves off from being available to God's action in our lives. In the biblical accounts of creation. we find the lure of an escape from the ordinary the root crisis of properly using our God-given freedom. The story of Lucifer and the fallen angels is a story of beings discontent with being ordinary. As they try to move beyond the ordinary by shutting out God, this becomes their hell. So, too, the story of Adam and Eve is a story of two people, in the freshness of human life, already desirous of escaping the ordinary—to be like gods.

Sacramentally we are reminded that God continues to take the ordinary—water, bread and wine, oil—to make extraordi-

Prisms for a Christ-Life

nary contact with us. Even when our prayer or the spirituality we live is—try as we may—ordinary, we thus have the very quality which allows it to become the vehicle of God's action. The difficulty for us in accepting the ordinary is not just from an inherent human tendency to want to be noticed and praised, but also from the graced impetus to strive, to struggle, to desire to grow beyond where we are. How are we to distinguish these spirits within us, distinguish between movements that would lead us to close ourselves off to God by our self-focus and movements whereby God is drawing us ever closer in our surrender?

As portrayed in the Gospels, Jesus had to spend a lot of his efforts both in his ordinary apostolic life and then again in his resurrected life to prove his ordinariness. He gets tired, he eats and drinks, he needs friends, and he takes time to pray—all ordinary activities for us humans. And yet it was in these very ordinary dealings that God is fully present to us in Jesus Christ. Perhaps the part of the church year we call "ordinary time" is a necessary reminder to us of how God wants to work with us.

Let Us Pray

**Shine your love on us each dawn
and gladden all our days.**

*You have been our haven, Lord,
from generation to generation.
Before the mountains existed,
before the earth was born,
from age to age you are God.*

*You return us to dust,
children of earth back to earth.
For in your eyes a thousand years
are like a single day:
They pass with the swiftness of sleep.*

You sweep away the years
as sleep passes at dawn,
like grass that springs up in the day
and is withered by evening.

Our life is a mere seventy years,
eighty with good health,
and all it gives us
is toil and distress;
then the thread breaks
and we are gone.

How long, O Lord, before you return?
Pity your servants,
shine your love on us each dawn,
and gladden all our days.

Balance our past sorrows
with present joys
and let your servants, young and old,
see the splendor of your work.
Let your loveliness shine on us,
and bless the work we do,
bless the work of our hands.

PSALM 90:1-6, 10, 13-17

Prisms for a Christ-Life

Devotion and Devotions

*F*or many Christians the month of May evokes memories of processions and crownings and songs in honor of Mary, Mother of God. In a similar way the month of June recalls the novenas and hymns and vigils devoted to the heart of Jesus.

Devotions, once such a bright part of our pre-Vatican II faith lives, now seem like faded fabrics preserved under some obscure museum's glass showcase. Although nostalgia may too readily find its place, we need to acknowledge how devotions in a pre-Vatican II church fired up the faith lives of many parish communities and the missionary zeal of many women and men. On the other hand, devotions, with their vernacular prayers and singable hymns, sometimes overshadowed even feast-day Masses in people's affection. In fact, the Mass itself often became the time and place for people's devotional practices while the priest quietly busied himself with the Latin prayers and formal ritual of the Mass.

Perhaps the greatest gift of the liturgical renewal of Vatican II was the clarity brought to the central place of liturgy, both the Eucharist and the Liturgy of the Hours. Devotions, as a result, were given the chance to take a more modestly proportioned place in our spiritual lives, sometimes even to die after years of devout usefulness. But at the same time that the Vatican II renewal was creating a spiritual renewal of prayer practices in correct proportion, a major shift in human interaction was taking place in the Western world and having undue influence upon some other nations. New cultural patterns of lifestyle, fragmentations of family living and of many a neighborhood, the suburban *driving* (not walking) distances between home and church, and the easy attractions of TV and home video entertainment every night of the week are among the reasons why the practice of devotions fell by the wayside. The majority of Catholics today have no experience of such devotional practices. The case is little different in the present-day worship and prayer lives of many men and women religious.

Devotions need once again to find their place in faith lives that too often merit the descriptive terms "thin" or "desiccated." There is no doubt that devotions bring color to our somewhat monochrome lives of worship. Devotions rouse some passion in a faith lived often too listlessly, even in Eucharists attended routinely. Yet devotions from the past need more than just a dusting off. They need to be rethought and reexpressed for our context and time. Even more importantly, perhaps, devotions need to be refounded on the essential of devotion itself.

Devotion in the Christian theological tradition is defined as "an ease in finding God." To say that "here we have a man or woman of devotion" is to point to someone who has an evident and easy relationship with God. To be a person of devotion is to be specially graced by God. Praying for devotion in our spiritual lives is essential for a healthy existence. Even our ministries receive special effectiveness from being permeated with devotion. Devotions and devotion are related something like the chicken and the egg. If we are people of devotion, we will find that our faith naturally tends to express itself in prayers to Jesus and to Mary and the saints, in vigils, in processions and pilgrimages, and in other such external forms. Devotions in their proper proportion feed and strengthen the Christian lives of all the faithful. Devotions cannot be absent from our faith expression without the loss of devotion itself.

Perhaps the time has come for all of us to reassess our need for devotions as the fuel and lifesource for the devoted lives we Christians desire to live.

Let Us Pray

**My whole being
is at rest in you, my God.**

*Lord, I am not proud,
holding my head too high,
reaching beyond my grasp.*

*No, I am calm and tranquil
like a weaned child
resting in its mother's arms:
my whole being at rest.*

*Let Israel rest in the Lord,
now and for ever.*

PSALM 131

Models for Living

Who are the people by whom you have been most influenced?

*M*any of us must at one time or another have tried to answer this question for ourselves or at the inquiry of others: Precisely which people have strongly influenced my life? Some may quickly name their fathers and mothers; others go on to name favorite teachers or special friends. Still others may name people in world affairs or in the worlds of sports, the arts, or medicine. Probably not very many of us spontaneously turn to the men and women whom the church has declared holy and named as outstanding members of the communion of saints. Yet the reason why the church calls our attention to these people is to allow us to see in other followers of Christ what we hope to become. Just as the church of the Eastern rites emphasizes icons that give us a glimpse of the world of the holy, so the Latin-rite church proposes the study of the lives of saints so that we may be inspired by them and formed and then moved along a path of holiness as Jesus' apostles.

Perhaps at one time many of us did not appreciate how the more medieval theology of mediators needed updating like so many time-bound ways of expressing our faith and its practices—the process mandated by Vatican II. Now it seems we recognize our need of—and so are more open to—the positive influence our fellow Christians, canonized or otherwise esteemed, can have on our lives. No longer do we, almost superstitiously, look to Mary or other chosen saints for special favors. Instead we take our direction from the Vatican II understanding and description of Mary's place in the communion of saints under the specially privileged titles of mother and first disciple. And so we look to our favorite men and women saints particularly in their relationship to us as brothers and sisters and as our fellow disciples. If Christians in general are exhibiting a greater need for this kind of influence in their devotional lives, even more might men and women religious look to the holy ones special to their congregations for living the kind of discipleship charismatically appropriate to their following of Christ. Whether it be the contemporary retelling of saints' lives or recapturing their spirit in new artistic portrayals or recovering prayers of theirs that are appropriate to our times—there still are ways for holy men and women to touch us in our daily living. We may more readily find light coming to us in dark moments of our experience from the uncovered lamp of these human lives than from any theoretical studies or documents. We may also find ourselves more energized for entering into the evangelizing mission of Jesus through the radiance of their inspiration and example.

Probably even more surprising than our slowness in naming saints as major influences in our lives is the not infrequent omission of even the name Jesus. As we enter into the Advent and Christmas seasons, maybe more fully than Jesus being "the reason for the season," we might say that the reason for the season is for us to remind ourselves that Jesus is *the* unique influence upon our lives all year long. Jesus is the one who has influenced how we live, how we pray, how we interact, how we die. Jesus is the one who calls us to a way of following; Jesus is the Teacher, and we all remain the lifelong learners, the ones in continuing formation. Perhaps we need to ask ourselves another question. Is it true that for us not to name Jesus as *the* great influence of our lives is more than just a memory slip? Does our answer uncover for us that our everyday busy lives are being spent on behalf of lesser gods than the God Incarnate? The question is worth more than a Christmastime reflection.

Let Us Pray

**Serve the Lord with gladness,
enter God's presence with joy!**

*Shout joy to the Lord, all earth,
serve the Lord with gladness,
enter God's presence with joy!*

*Know that the Lord is God,
our maker to whom we belong,
our shepherd, and we the flock.*

*Enter the temple gates,
the courtyard with thanks and praise;
give thanks and bless God's name.*

*Indeed the Lord is good!
God's love is for ever,
faithful from age to age.*

PSALM 100

Divine Questions

Questions play an important part in our biblical tradition. The first question presented in the Bible is the one which God directs to us human beings, "Where are you?" In the Gospels, Jesus' question "Who do you say that I am?" demands a response from every Christian, perhaps more than once in a lifetime. "Woman, why are you weeping? Who is it you are looking for?" challenges us in our sorrow and our disappointments. "Simon, son of John, do you love me?" pricks the conscience of sinner and saint alike.

Not all questions are neatly answered. For example, "How does one pray?" and "How does one love?" have pieces of answers which together make up a simple but intricate mosaic that stretches as far as human experience can reach. Jesus, in trying to share with us his experience of God, seemed to be most at home in everyday images of the living world around us and in the parables, which capture some basic human experience writ large. Who does not remember a woman sweeping a house for a lost coin? That is the way God searches out each of us in our lost moments. Who has not been touched by a story of a person robbed and left half-dead by the roadside and various passers-by, among whom there is one who cares? From such a parable, we all know a little better what it means to be neighbor. Stories, symbols, and images become so often the prisms whereby we gain new or fresh insight into some of our deepest human and divine realities.

It is true that questions sometimes only lead to

Prisms for a Christ-Life

more questions. But questions also lead to ways of responding that affect the direction of our lives and our ministry. Some questions can truly affect our relationship with God, with our fellow men and women, and with our world. The God who asks questions is also a God of surprises.

Let Us Pray

Send your light and truth, my God.

Why have you forgotten me?
Why am I bent double
under the weight of enemies?

Send your light and truth.
They will escort me
to the holy mountain
where you make your home.

I will approach the altar of God,
God, my highest joy,
and praise you with the harp,
God, my God.

Why are you sad, my heart?
Why do you grieve?
Wait for the Lord.
I will yet praise God my savior.

PSALM 43

Heroic Living

*P*ope John Paul II has set records in saint making. In his various missionary travels, he frequently celebrates the ritual of beatification or canonization of a woman or man recognized for holiness by the local people. Some are critical of this making of saints. "Out of step with the times," they say. Others just wonder why.

We human beings need our heroes and heroines. The stories of women and men who have captured our minds and hearts because of their bravery, their dedicated service, their contribution to a more humane world have been told in every culture and in every age. The names change, the circumstances differ, but the inspiration for human living remains the same.

We all seem to be searching for a glimpse or two of heroism not too far from home. Yet some fear or some reluctance appears to stifle, early on, our own desire for the heroic. Various factors may contribute to this reluctance. Perhaps pop psychology, too readily imbibed as gospel, has made us too content with being the ordinary persons we are, too willing to be coddled into a generic self-esteem. Or when heroes are proposed, a mean spirit in us and in our culture may drive us to search out ways to cut these people back down to ordinary size . . . or less. Maybe such behavior flows from a poorly idealized proletarian spirit which is a communist residue in us all. Often it seems that heroes or heroines are quickly raised up and just as quickly forgotten. Perhaps our enthusiasm for their example and their deeds lasts no longer than the music or video of the moment. Then, too, we probably fear the disappointment of the hero or heroine letting us down; we surely fear the cost of heroism for ourselves.

Despite such stifling factors or because of them, our need for inspiring heroism to permeate our everyday world in the living example of contemporary women and men remains. The various spiritual traditions in the church have been first enfleshed in the lives of women and men before they came to be written down as programs for the following of Christ. Life and ministry shone out in persons with names and faces before any religious rule or constitutions were formulated. There comes a time in every spirituality when structures or formulas or written theological treatises are essential if it is to become a heritage or tradition within the church community. A common way that particular spiritualities have been institutionalized has been through the foundation of religious congregations. Religious life does not exist as a generic reality, but only in particular embodiments, each with its own approved rule of life, an organized spiritual tradition. A religious rule of life, then, not only provides for the identity of a particular religious family as a legitimate form of following Christ, but also brings that family's prophetic voice to the harmonies and counterpoints of the church on earth. The danger of any heritage arises when it becomes a tomb or sculpted sarcophagus, beautiful in its form, but containing disconnected bones devoid of breath. Only heroes and heroines make spiritualities live.

Can people live heroic lives in an unheroic age? The answer obviously lies with us. No matter what our spirituality or heritage may be, the people who embody it for us retain an importance beyond a brilliant theoretical study of a particular charism or some wonderfully fashioned new constitutions. Saints, both old and new, hold out to us the promise that *this* kind of a following of Christ is humanly possible. Requiring a little heroism, perhaps, but humanly possible.

Our church and our world need heroes and heroines. Anyone of us who is serious about the spiritual heritage we try to live recognizes the call within it to be heroic. To paraphrase Chesterton, it is not so much that heroism has been tried in our day and found wanting; rather, today we try so little to be heroic.

Let Us Pray

**Bless God, house of Israel;
sing God's name, our delight.**

*Your name lives for ever, Lord,
your renown never fades,
for you give your people justice
and attend to their needs.*

*Pagan idols are silver and gold
crafted by human hands.
Their mouths cannot speak,
their eyes do not see.*

*Their ears hear nothing,
their nostrils do not breathe.
Their makers who rely on them
become like these hollow images.*

*Bless God, house of Israel,
house of Aaron, house of Levi,
every faithful one.*

*Blest be the Lord of Zion,
who calls Jerusalem home.
Hallelujah!*

PSALM 135:13-21

Communion of the Holy

*P*ope John Paul II has declared more men and women blessed and canonized saints than any of his predecessors in the papacy. He himself has explained his action by saying that we are more than ever in need of many models—some from within our countries or cultures, others closer in time—to aid us in our own Christian living.

We also might suspect that the need for recognition of holy women and men as models and helps for our life is heightened by the individualism that has become embedded in our United States culture and similar cultures. When we move about in a cultural individualism, there is a tendency to make even our faith an individual conquest. "I" will save my soul—of course, with Jesus' saving grace. But still it is "my" effort.

From the very beginning of the Christian community, St. Paul stressed the importance of our being a communion of saints. Although Paul's Greek word *koinonia* is rendered by the English *fellowship* more often than the English *communion*, the idea cannot be mistaken. Paul's conversion experience on the road to Damascus would never let him waver from the conviction that the (persecuted) Christians' union together with Christ is so intimate that Jesus can say "I am Jesus, the one you are persecuting." That same experience roots the Pauline image of the Body of Christ in which all Christians are members, differing in gifts and functions, but all being necessary for the healthy functioning of the Body.

The reality that we need to hold on to today is the truth that "we all need one another." The communion of saints reminds us of this fact. As it has developed over time, the communion of saints refers first to us baptized and now living our seemingly humdrum lives within our church communities. The communion of saints means also those who have died and are officially recognized by the church as the holy ones giving example for us. The communion of saints includes finally those who have died—sometimes identified as the "souls in purgatory"—many of whom we remember dearly and who for their part still remain caring and concerned for us. The fullness of the meaning of the communion of saints keeps all of us caring and concerned for one another—in our union with Christ and in the power of the Spirit.

In our creed we profess that we believe in the "*sanctorum communio*"—that is, not only a union among holy people but also a people made holy by their participation (*communio*) in holy things (the sacraments). Today we are being called to put that belief into action. In our remembering those who have died, both the recognized saints and those everyday ones of our families and friends, we are joined in a conversation—a special conversation that has been traditionally called *prayer*—praying for one another! We need to be aware of the stories of their lives so that we can know and feel their strength and their compassion and their *receiving* of God's grace through participation in the sacramental life. We, the now-members of this church on earth, must hold one another in prayer, both public liturgical and personal private, and reach out with helpful hands to one another because we are in communion, the union of holy ones sustained by holy things. We are not alone; we live our life of faith in communion.

Let Us Pray

**Bless the Lord,
all who serve in God's house.**

*Bless the Lord,
all who serve in God's house,
who stand watch
throughout the night.*

*Lift up your hands
in the holy place
and bless the Lord.*

*And may God,
the maker of earth and sky,
bless you from Zion.*

PSALM 134

Working at Virtuous Living

*W*e do not talk much about "working at the virtuous life." Perhaps the Pelagian inference—that "working at it" is enough, all by itself—keeps us suspicious of such talk. Maybe we are reluctant to admit explicitly that virtue is on our list of outmoded things. There is also the possibility, even the likelihood, that some people strong in virtue have offended us in some way. "Nice" people may be easier to live with and less offensive than people imbued with courage or fired up for justice' sake. But Jesus demands more of his followers than that they be nice. Christians in every age need to work at the virtuous life.

In North America the news media made and still make much of various accusations or admissions of sexual misconduct by bishops, priests, and religious. The result was that the leadership in the local church and in religious congregations had the painful, but necessary, task of coming to terms with a difficult and disturbing situation. What becomes evident to those living the consecrated life is that celibate chastity is not only something which we can "lose," but also something to be worked at: that only through a lifetime effort does one grow in chastity and love. Various programs like Marriage Encounter and the Christian Family Movement and Teams of Our Lady have long stressed how couples need to work at their marital chastity if they are going to deepen their love and grow to be ever more faithful to each other. In a similar way, through some painful reminders today, both men and women in celibate commitment are being called to make the effort they need to make if they are to grow as loving celibate people.

In the scholastic theology of St. Thomas Aquinas, we are taught the meaning of the virtues of the Christian life through his masterly explanation of habit. It would be interpreting Thomas fairly to bring our commonsense thinking about acquiring a habit to our understanding of his insight into acquiring—"working at"—virtue. Without denying the primacy of grace, especially experienced in the theological virtues of faith, hope, and charity, we need to put forth the human effort to make those qualities more deeply our own.

Theological developments since Vatican II have stressed that, just as conversion is continual in a Christian's life, so too growth in virtue is never finished—nor can either of these occur in isolation; they demand the presence of the faith community. Similarly, we now see even more clearly that virtue, like conversion, is never a private matter but impacts the public and social sphere. Our very working at virtue gives force to our evangelizing efforts in our families, communities, and workplaces.

As a case in point, then, there are recent efforts being made to work at celibate chastity within a community setting and not in isolation. As married people have discovered in their various Christian family organizations, it is within the faith community that growth in virtue finds its support and that marriage and family values are witnessed to and witnessed. All of us need to "work at" virtue today.

Let Us Pray

**You, O Lord, are close;
your law is my whole truth.**

*My heart begs you, Lord:
hear me, so I can keep faith.
I beg you, make me free,
so I can live your laws.*

I face you in the cold night
praying, waiting for your word.
I keep watch through the night,
repeating what you promise.

Hear me, loving God,
let your justice make me live.
The wicked close in on me;
to them your law is foreign.

But you, Lord, are closer still,
your law is my whole truth,
learned when I was young,
fixed for all time.

PSALM 119:145-152

Prisms for a Christ-Life

Exploring Faith Practice

*T*wo opposing tendencies vie within us from the very beginning of life. Human beings are described as always struggling to stay within the comfort life of the womb and yet pushing to find a continuing newness of life outside the womb. We rejoice in the known, the familiar, what has always been, the traditional. We can be enlivened also by the unknown, what is new and untried, the innovative. A healthy passage between these two human tendencies is caught up in the activity called exploration. Our growth as children came through exploration; we grow as adults only if we continue regularly to experience the exploratory passage, a passage that joins the past to the future.

When John Paul II made his appeal for a new evangelization, it was an exploratory call. It was not immediately evident to all of us Catholics how far this call extended. We are beginning to realize that a new evangelization takes in not just ways of proclaiming the gospel that are effective for our time but also ways of celebrating that proclamation. The latest revisioning of the sacramentary and lectionary is a part of this continuing renewal of our efforts in celebrating the Eucharist as the source and summit of the Christian life. We continue to explore the passage between the liturgical rites as we have known them and a new formulation of these rites that may more effectively help today's people understand their meaning in relation to contemporary patterns of thought and expectation.

A liturgical spirituality rightly has pride of place. But so-called "popular" devotions are important too. In the Roman

Catholic Latin rite, expression found in liturgical prayer usually remains formal, with feelings restricted and subjective emotions set aside—whatever the vernacular translation. The more personal and emotive piety that was characteristic of Catholic devotional life in the 19th and 20th centuries—expressed in popular language and images—necessarily had to recede in importance after Vatican Council II. The explorations central to our faith expression in baptism, Eucharist, and reconciliation focused all of our worshiping energy. Marian devotions, Sacred Heart devotions, Eucharistic holy hours, and Stations of the Cross suffered a time of eclipse. Granted that the central place of the Eucharistic celebration and the other sacraments has been properly positioned for us Catholics, we are now enabled to express our persistent hunger and need to nourish our Catholic life also in nonliturgical or, perhaps more positively, more personal and popular ways. As an integral part of our actively entering into our new evangelization, we need to explore devotions that do not seem to be relics of the past, but rather are "new" prayerful ways of celebrating our faith that express the yearnings of our hearts today.

What form will these explorations take? We cannot say since devotional life is so much shaped by the social and cultural milieu in which we live. Devotions need contemporary imaging, vocal expressions, and musical or quasi-musical rhythms that appeal to today's people. For example, does the May procession and crowning of Mary as queen—a memory many Catholics treasure—emphasize rather the distancing of Mary from our daily experience rather than her closeness? What may have been "devotional" at a particular time may not be a fitting expression and imaging today. Does a 40-hour Eucharistic devotion fit the rhythm of our social milieu or would a 7 p.m.-to-12 midnight or a 24-hour, all-night vigil speak better? We need to explore how these "old" devotions can be truly a part of our new evangelization; our exploration is an effort to stretch personal and group memories into personal and group hopes and expressions.

We may look to the renewal of some of our older devotions such as the devotion to the Sacred Heart (identified of old with the month of June) or we may seek to honor and find our own life-inspiration by devotions expressed for one of our newly canonized saints who combines charity with a prophetic thirst for justice. Regardless, we are responding to the call for a new evangelization. Exploration is necessary for a faith that is alive and well. No, better said, exploration is necessary for us believers who want to grow in our maturity in Christ.

Let Us Pray

**From morning watch until night,
I waited for the Lord.**

*From the depths I call to you,
Lord, hear my cry.
Catch the sound of my voice
raised up, pleading.*

*If you record our sins,
Lord, who could survive?
But because you forgive
we stand in awe.*

*I trust in God's word,
I trust in the Lord.
More than sentries for dawn
I watch for the Lord.*

*More than sentries for dawn
let Israel watch.
The Lord will bring mercy
and grant full pardon.
The Lord will free Israel
from all its sins.*

PSALM 130

Discerning Enough

*W*hen is "enough" enough? It is the common question: Did you get enough to eat? enough to drink? Is the room warm (cool) enough for you?

Enough is a hard concept to define in our practical living. If people's perception of their own worth as persons is tied up in their work, when have they worked long enough or hard enough? Some people find it difficult to turn over responsibility to others or "to retire." *Enough* seems not to have a place in their vocabulary. Others at a younger age let work consume their days and evenings and weekends. They, too, seem oblivious to the possibility of freely chosen limits. We have heard the phrase "get a life" and we know that it can be a criticism to the quick for such people.

Besides questions of food and drink and work and rest, *enough* plays a similarly difficult role in determining security. When are there more lights outside and more locks and alarm systems than we need for reasonable security? When do we have enough money for travel and its surprises and emergencies? When is there enough money put aside for care of the elderly— others or ourselves? The danger with a money-focus is, as Jesus describes in a story, that our barns are never quite big enough to hold our piled-up wealth.

When we consider healthcare in the industrialized countries, we find again the difficulty of knowing when enough medical care has been called upon and when we are moving into extraordinary and sometimes minimally enhancing medical procedures. The subtlety of *enough* allows us morally to steer our way between the always immoral assisted suicide and the decision to refuse any extraordinary means to prolong life.

For each of us, in our uniqueness, to know how to live enough and move enough and have being enough remains a rich grace-gift to be prayed for. We call the gift which helps us to say "enough" Christian discernment. To be a person who discerns demands that we be people attuned to the working of God's Spirit in our lives. Discernment is not a process of decision making that we stir up on a moment's whim. When we think of people (perhaps including ourselves) as being attuned to God, we mean that they have a serious and ongoing relationship with God in prayer and in reflecting on the Scriptures and God's workings in the world. Such people find themselves growing in a sensitivity, as all lovers do, to the ways of seeing, the desires, and the ways of acting of the one loved. That kind of sensitivity is the power source of our Christian discernment. Because sensitivity is involved, it is not something we learn by rulebooks although Jesus reminds us that "I have come, not to abolish [the law and the prophets], but to fulfill them" (Mt 5:17). As we can appreciate, the process of discerning is not a sometime thing that we can blithely manage at short notice unless we are sensitized lovers of God. The dailyness of prayer and Eucharist are privileged ways for us becoming lovers growing in sensitivity.

Today we seem to live with the question of *Enough?* in many areas of our lives, and our personal decision about *enough* does not come easy. We need to enter deeply into our Catholic faith and experience Jesus' promise of "another Paraclete." Yet there is one instance of *enough* which remains a paradox. Can we ever grow enough in God's love that our sensitivity for discernment can say "enough"?

Let Us Pray

My whole life, give praise to God.

Praise the Lord, my heart!
My whole life, give praise.
Let me sing to God
as long as I live.

Never depend on rulers:
born of earth, they cannot save.
They die, they turn to dust.
That day, their plans crumble.

They are wise who depend on God,
who look to Jacob's Lord,
creator of heaven and earth,
maker of the teeming sea.

The Lord keeps faith for ever,
giving food to the hungry,
justice to the poor,
freedom to captives.

The Lord opens blind eyes
and straightens the bent,
comforting widows and orphans,
protecting the stranger.
The Lord loves the just
but blocks the path of the wicked.

Zion, praise the Lord!
Your God reigns for ever,
from generation to generation.
Hallelujah!

PSALM 146

Prisms for a Christ-Life

Pausing for Life

There are times in our life which provide us with the occasion for a pause—a time for assessment, for evaluation, for celebration, for gratitude.

We have so many of these "pauses" built into our ordinary life that we can forget how important their place is for the healthy living of life, including the spiritual. The changing seasons of the year, with their cycles of growth and dormancy, present one rhythmic pattern observed in religious practices of people through the centuries. As we quantify the rhythm of a day into our minutes and hours and then measure further into days of a week and weeks of a month and months of a year, we are struck at how we humanly have built so many pauses into our ordinary living. As a matter of fact, we humans are not meant to be "energerizer bunnies" (as in a famous TV ad about a brand of battery) that just keep going and going, always doing more of the same. No, we are people who have waking and sleeping patterns, who enjoy times of work and of recreation, who seek out periods of solitude and of social interaction, who are marked by successes and failures and those many "gray-area" projects whose value remains unclear. We are meant to pause, to be a reflective people, because we are formed by the Bible—that very reflectively written account of God's dealings with his people. We Christians are a people who appreciate the flow of a liturgical year, with its celebratory pauses that bring home in ever new ways the key moments of our faith-life with God.

Though there are these many natural and ecclesial pauses in

our life, we seem to be unwilling to choose such a rhythm in our personal daily living. Both in our personal life and in our parish or community projects, we often do not take time to set and identify some intermediate goals. We rush on, instead of reflecting on what we have done up to this point, on what changes might be desirable, on how much gratitude we should have and express for all the cooperation we have received, and perhaps on what mistakes we have made and whose feelings we may have bruised. We Christians need to make time to reflect, to assess and celebrate and apologize, as our way of working with God. We need to choose to build this kind of pause into our day (like the Ignatian daily awareness examen) and into the works and projects we are busy on in concert with others. In community we need to choose to build in these pauses so that community life and community projects can make wise choices and avoid sad crises. If we choose to make "anniversary-like pauses" ordinary and so build them into our daily life, we will discover a power source that makes for a physically, psychologically, and spiritually healthy life.

Perhaps we all need to look for timely occasions when we can pause—to celebrate, to assess, to correct, to revitalize for the continuing effort. By such choices, we grow into being the reflective Christians God's word calls us to be. We meet God, in his gift of time to us, by pausing to appreciate it and use it well.

Let Us Pray

**How I begged and you healed me, God;
for ever I will thank you.**

*Celebrate, all you saints,
praise this awesome God,
whose anger passes quickly,
whose mercy lasts a lifetime—
as laughter fills a day
after one brief night of tears.*

143

When all was going well,
I though I could never fall;
with God's powerful blessing,
I would stand like a mountain!
Then you hid your face;
I shook with fear!

I cried out, "Lord, Lord!"
I begged, I pleaded:
"What good is my blood to you?
Why push me down the pit?
Can dead bones praise you,
recount your unbroken love?
Listen to me, O God,
turn and help me now."

You changed my anguish
into this joyful dance,
pulled off my sackcloth,
gave me bright new robes,
that my life might sing your glory,
never silent in your praise.
For ever I will thank you,
O Lord my God.

PSALM 30:5-13

Reverence for Life

For those of us living in the midwestern part of the United States, the spring and early summer seasons bless us with a burst of flowering trees and shrubs and a continuing array of nature's living variety. Obviously all these signs of life are not created out of nothing each year. In fact, the changing seasons remind us of how much life remains hidden from our daily human perspective.

Seeds look to be so dry and lifeless. Even in planting them in lawn or garden, we can only wonder about and wait for the activities of life still hidden from our sight. Oceans appear to our eyes as only a huge volume of water, but oceans teem with life—mostly hidden beneath the surface—which marine biologists endlessly discover and observe and marvel at.

If we buy into the impressions promoted by contemporary advertising, we find ourselves acting as if what we see is what life is all about. Life as sold by secular culture seems to bankrupt itself in surface impressions. Just how limited such a vision of life is quickly becomes apparent when we deal with moral and religious issues of human living. Abortion only becomes an option if people keep human life out of sight. Arguments for abortion deal with choices and rights, with nary a thought about the hiddenness of human life. "Ethnic cleansing," whether it be in Europe, Africa, Asia, or America, is a cosmetic phrase to disguise the deadly idea that some peoples are more deserving of life than others. Put into practice, this deadly idea joins the age-old slave trading, the Nazi concentration camps, and futuristic scientific cloning as another sadly and horrendously narrow human mishandling of human life. For all the words about environment and ecology and quality of human life, we seem unable to reverence the mystery of life—visible life and hidden life—with which our world abounds.

For the young Christian community at Colossae, St. Paul used the pregnant phrase that "our life is hidden now with Christ in God." Perhaps we need to reflect more on the hiddenness of our faith life and thereby come to an appreciation and reverence for the hiddenness of life in general. The fledgling Christian community at Colossae realized that in everyday life they looked pretty much the same as everyone else. They ate, they drank, they sometimes went hungry, they married and had families, they got sick, they died; they had joys and sorrows. They gathered, of course, for Eucharist, and their concern and care for one another and anyone in need did give them some mark of distinctiveness. But overall they lived with a new reverence for life—from the very young to the very old. Why? Because the risen Christ in whom they all were baptized had brought them into a new relationship to God and to one another—a relationship subtle as the Spirit but as real as the risen Christ himself. As Saul (now Paul the writer) experienced and many other persecutors have learned since his day, a voice insists that it is Jesus whom they persecute. We Christians hear Jesus insisting, "If you do it to the least of these, my brothers and sisters, you are doing it to me." We touch here the source of the hidden life we all live in Christ.

But Jesus does more than affect the hiddenness of human relationships—whatever tribe or nationality, religious affiliation or secular lifestyle. Because Jesus has taken on the darkness and hiddenness of suffering and death and by his rising joined it into a new fullness of life, the physical world in which we live is not the same as it was. Suffering and death are not just problems to be solved and if possible eliminated; suffering and death, now seen in a wholly new relationship to life in the risen Christ, must also be met with reverence. In the midst of all our necessary human efforts to relieve the suffering in our world, we believers stand with reverence before suffering, for we know with the sureness of faith that because of Christ life lies hidden even in suffering, sometimes especially in suffering.

Therein, deep down, like life in winter, lives Christian joy and the root of Christian reverence for life.

Let Us Pray

Lovers of justice, shout joy to the Lord.

Shout joy to the Lord,
lovers of justice,
how right to praise!
Praise God on the harp,
with ten-string lyre
sing to the Lord.

For the word of the Lord is true:
what God says, God does.
This lover of truth and justice
fills the earth with love.

The Lord looks down
and sees our human kind.
From heaven God surveys
all peoples on earth.
The maker of human hearts
knows every human act.

God keeps a loving eye
on all who believe,
on those who count on God
to bring relief from famine,
to rescue them from death.

With all we are, we wait for God,
the Lord, our help, our shield.
Our hearts find joy in the Lord;
we trust God's holy name.
Love us, Lord!
We wait for you.

PSALM 33:1-2, 4-5, 13-15, 18-22

Prisms for a Christ-Life

Prophets

"What did you go out to the desert to see? A prophet?"
(Luke 7:26)

*T*he question which Jesus asked his own people takes on a special poignancy for us today in the church. Our biblical tradition indicates that God raises up prophetic people in dark and difficult days. Because many see the time of renewal called for by Vatican II as a period of continuing struggle and tension—sometimes sadly with positions defended or fixed rather than with dialogue explored—affecting people and priests in parishes, bishops in national hierarchies, and religious in the same congregation, there is a greater tendency today to go running out, searching for a prophet. As usual there is also the temptation for some to play the prophet.

But the prophetic tradition strongly emphasizes that true prophets do not identify the role for themselves. God plucks people out of ordinary circumstances, evokes some kind of personal conversion, and then speaks and works through them, even in their own reluctance for the role, and in their fear and trembling. Although we tend to apply the word *prophet* glibly to some modern-day leaders, educators, and writers, we perhaps are not far off the mark when we search for those movements and calls of God that come in incremental ways through ordinary-looking people and events. It is to acknowledge that prophets, like saints, have a range from "capital P" prophets (like our canonized "capital S" saints) with a major message of modeling and influence to the almost hidden (because of everydayness) small-letter prophets who in limited and confined ways raise questions, suggest new directions, make us uncomfortable, and at the same time give us hope. Prophets of lasting influence are scarce at any time in our world's history. Yet we may find it all too easy, even now, to mute the "small p" prophet either in our fixated search for major prophetic voices or in our disdain for less-than-radical calls. The even greater loss, however, happens when we may intentionally or unintentionally downplay our own lived (small p) prophetic witness to Christ's values—an integral part of our own chosen way of life.

Perhaps, in our effort to identify prophets, no truer discernment or greater tribute can be given to any prophet, spelled with large or small p, than to be identified, like Moses, as a faithful servant of God.

Let Us Pray

**Let the coastland and its people
fill the world with praise.**

*Sing the Lord a new song.
Let the sea and its creatures,
the coastland and its people
fill the world with praise.*

*Let every village and town,
from Kedar on the plain
to Sela in the hills,
take up the joyful song.
Sing glory to the Lord,
give praise across the world.*

*The Lord strides like a hero
who rouses fury
with a great battle cry
and charges against the enemy.*

"I have kept quiet too long,
too long held back.
Like a woman in labor
I now scream and cry out:

"I will lay waste mountains and hills
and stunt all their greenery.
I will dry up rivers and pools
and create an arid wasteland.

"I will lead the blind safely
along strange roads.
I will make their darkness light,
their winding ways straight.
I will do all this,
I will not fail them."

ISAIAH 42:10-16

To Walk Justly

*J*ustice is a necessary part of our living a Christian life. With so much evident injustice in our civil society, injustice paradoxically in our justice systems, and even apparent injustice in our divine and all-too-human church, we can appreciate a reexamination for ourselves about our response to God's call to walk justly.

For justice is a tricky concept. We often identify justice with a balance sheet. We hear "an eye for an eye, a tooth for a tooth" not as a statement of vengeance, but as our own words for our idea of justice. And Jesus clearly said that such an interpretation of justice has no connection with the way God sees life. Justice based on rights, justice based on equal balances, may approach a good philosopher's or civil libertarian's idea of justice. But it is perhaps no more than the threshold of a Christian understanding of justice. To paraphrase a Hopkins-like expression, too often "justice injustices."

When we struggle and fight for rights for the oppressed, who will be the new oppressed of our efforts? When we bully our way to see justice done, who will be trampled in the process? As we fight to provide life for some, what others are having to face a dying? Religious, in trying to fulfill a prophetic role in today's church, have made fresh claims on justice as their mission. But the question remains whether in their justice efforts they have been more often a stimulus for the increase of injustice.

God's justice, the gospel justice, is not a simple matter of securing rights and seeking a balance of scales, as we see depicted in our classical justice statues. The justice that Jesus describes deals with a turning the other cheek, with a giving of my cloak, with a walking of an extra mile. Justice is more identified with compassion, the compassion of a father who looks for his wayward child and rushes out to greet him and welcome him home with a celebration.

This understanding of justice finds a very narrow gateway into the human heart. We seem to be only at the threshold of realizing that there is today no such thing as a just war—if ever there was such a possibility. With great difficulty we, especially in the United States, are slow in realizing that capital punishment is not an act of justice. It more represents vengeance and sullies even further and makes less human those who advocate its use. With an abundance of lawyers, our society has not become more just but rather more litigious. Absorbing this kind of culture, even we followers of Jesus quickly claim rights, less so responsibilities. We see justice with an individual eye; common good is no longer an horizon of vision, even religiously. Are not we Catholics, especially women and men religious, called to be agents of communion in such a culture?

An agent of communion, making God's justice alive in the world, will come to understand why the cross is a paradoxical sign of justice. The cross remains the sign of human justice—the result of a human court calling for the death of an innocent Jewish man. The cross remains God's symbol of justice—allowing arms to be stretched wide to the left and to the right in an everlasting gesture of reconciliation. Working in Jesus' name, the agent of communion, the ambassador of reconciliation, will find the cross integral to living and promoting gospel justice.

The call that we hear, then, is not for the simple biblical jubilee justice of all properties being restored to the original owners of fifty years ago. It is not a call to a justice of the balance sheet. The call to which we Christians are challenged to respond puts our feet into the footprints of Jesus. If we are to walk justly with our God, we need to be people who know how to talk earnestly with others along the way. We call it dialogue. We need to be people who can negotiate. We need to be people who seek reconciliation. We need to be a people who act like Christ. As agents of communion, we seek to live a gospel justice.

Let Us Pray

**God's love is from all ages,
God's justice beyond all time.**

*The Lord, who works justice
and defends the oppressed,
teaches Moses and Israel
divine ways and deeds.*

*The Lord is tender and caring,
slow to anger, rich in love.
God will not accuse us long,
nor bring our sins to trial,
nor exact from us in kind
what our sins deserve.*

*As high as heaven above earth,
so great is God's love for believers.
As far as east from west,
so God removes our sins.*

*As tender as father to child,
so gentle is God to believers.
The Lord knows how we are made,
remembers we are dust.*

*Our days pass by like grass,
our prime like a flower in bloom.
A wind comes, the flower goes,
empty now its place.*

*God's love is from all ages,
God's justice beyond all time
for believers of each generation:
those who keep the covenant,
who take care to live the law.*

PSALM 103:6-18

Forgiveness

Forgiveness is not unknown in various religious traditions, but it holds central place in Christianity. The one truly Christian prayer—the prayer common to all Christians—is the Our Father as taught by Jesus. In this prayer, the only phrase that interrelates God's action and our own is forgiveness. "Forgive us our trespasses as we forgive those who trespass against us."

Forgiveness does not come easy to us. It is hard for us to ask for forgiveness. Moreover, while God is ever ready to forgive, we do not so readily find other persons forgiving us when we express our sorrow and our desire to be forgiven. From those who seek forgiveness, others may ask more—the fulfillment of this or that condition, the probation of longer time, a retribution that demands something beyond the debt incurred—before they even consider forgiving us. In the United States, the inmates on death row may truly be contrite and seek forgiveness, but the state and those offended still demand punishment, the punishment even of death. If we limit ourselves to a justice system, there is little place for forgiveness, whether it is the justice formally imposed by a secular judicial system or informally exercised by us in our day-to-day familial and more general social interactions.

The worldly social context in which we are immersed makes it difficult, then, for us to forgive as well as to seek forgiveness. The difficulty goes beyond the individual seeking forgiveness or the individual offering forgiveness. Each one is involved in the decision made regardless of the other individual involved. We know that we may seek, even beg, forgiveness and meet a stony heart. We also know that we may offer forgiveness, but we may be met by the turning away of the offending party. Regardless, the beauty of the grace of forgiveness remains for the one seeking to forgive or to be forgiven, even when it is not reciprocated.

Above and beyond the difficulty of a forgiving attitude is the true wonder of reconciliation. For reconciliation to happen, which is beyond forgiveness, it takes two—both parties active and, in a way, passive as well. From the first moment in the pursuit of reconciliation, a cooperation, a working together, is necessary. That forgiveness should be an integral part of our everyday Christian living is presumed. But, as St. Paul imaged it, our real work as Christians is the work of reconciliation. We are given by God the "ministry of reconciliation" (2 Co 5:18). In such a ministry, we will know the demands of dialogue, and we will experience the fatigue of negotiation. But this effort is required if we are to act as ambassadors of reconciliation.

We find ourselves called as Christians to live, with renewed effort, the forgiveness that must be an integral part of our life with Christ. But more, we step forward to work at a special responsibility within our Christian vocation: to be a people committed to laboring for reconciliation. In a world, in a nation, in a church, in parish life, in family life, in community life, we have much to do if we are to work at being ambassadors of reconciliation.

Let Us Pray

Lord, I give myself to you.

I trust you, God;
do not fail me,
nor let my enemies gloat.
No one loyal is shamed,
but traitors know disgrace.

Teach me how to live,
Lord, show me the way.
Steer me toward your truth,
you, my saving God,
you, my constant hope.

Recall your tenderness,
your lasting love.
Remember me, not my faults,
the sins of my youth.
To show your own goodness,
God, remember me.

Good and just is the Lord,
guiding those who stray.
God leads the poor,
pointing out the path.

God's ways are faithful love
for those who keep the covenant.
Be true to your name, O Lord,
forgive my sin, though great.

PSALM 25:2-11

Hospitality

*H*ospitality has become a popular theme recently in the commentaries of scripture scholars and in the books of current spiritual writers. Perhaps the popularity is a reactive response to the individualism prevalent in contemporary culture, to the isolating security measures in the face of crime, and to the anonymity of suburbia or apartment living. But stressing hospitality is not a contemporary creation. Hospitality as a theme runs through both Old and New Testament writings. Hospitality describes succinctly the double commandment of love of God and love of neighbor.

Hospitality has two aspects: being at home oneself and making another feel at home. There is an old saying: Home is were the heart is. Home may be connected with certain physical surroundings, but location is not the focus of being "at home." Any place can become home for us when our heart finds its rest there. When we make others feel at home, we have welcomed them in such a way that, by being with us, they find rest at their heart's center. Welcoming the other, welcoming the stranger, may often seem to put the focus only on the object of hospitality. But welcoming involves relationship. It takes two—the one being hospitable and the one receiving hospitality—and it is for both to experience that "home" is being shared because the hearts of both parties are involved.

The incident of Jesus' enjoying the hospitality of Martha and Mary in Luke's Gospel (10:38-42) has traditionally led to an interpretation of personality types labeled as Marthas or Marys

157

or to an interpretation of the alternative religious orientations of active and contemplative life. Perhaps greater insight into our Christian and Catholic living will be gained if we view both Martha and Mary under the lens of hospitality. Martha is certainly esteemed by biblical tradition for being busy about the efforts of making another feel at home. Mary, for her part, is praised by Jesus in the provocative expression of "choosing the better part" for making him feel so much at home. Together Martha and Mary represent the essentials of hospitality.

Mary, listening to Jesus and sitting at his feet, symbolizes the stance of every disciple. She finds her home in God, and her heart is at rest. She has the more essential quality (the "better part"), because she is at home in the deepest part of herself with God. Knowing her true home, she is empowered to offer hospitality to others. Martha represents the other essential quality of hospitality—the work of seeking out and actively inviting others to find a home. Hospitality is the practice which images our living the one commandment of love of God and neighbor.

The exercise of hospitality in our personal interaction with friends and strangers, in our religious community, and in our parish life provides us today in our times and cultures with the sign similar to the one distinguishing the first Christians: "See how they love one another." In the midst of the contentiousness that we often find in our dealings with people who differ with us or who are different from us, we are called to live a hospitality that remains true to our biblical tradition and to the best that is in human hearts. Hospitality becomes the expression on the faces of people seeing Christ in one another.

Let Us Pray

I will bless you, Lord my God!

I will bless you, Lord my God!
You fill the world with awe.
You dress yourself in light,

in rich, majestic light.
You stretched the sky like a tent,
built your house beyond the rain.
You ride upon the clouds,
the wind becomes your wings,
the storm becomes your herald,
your servants, bolts of light.

You feed springs that feed brooks,
rushing down ravines,
water for wild beasts,
for wild asses to drink.
Birds nest nearby
and sing among the leaves.

You drench the hills
with rain from high heaven.
You nourish the earth
with what you create.

You make grass grow for cattle,
make plants grow for people,
food to eat from the earth
and wine to warm the heart,
oil to glisten on faces
and bread for bodily strength.

God, how fertile your genius!
You shape each thing,
you fill the world
with what you do.

PSALM 104:1-4, 10-15, 24

Prisms for a Christ-Life

The Prism of Religious Life

Religious life today presents a varied landscape of images. Some would see the landscape more in the fading light of autumn colors or, perhaps, far more somberly in the gray bleakness of a barren wintertime. Others look out and observe a springtime of new growth, with tender fresh green shoots and small delicate blossoms just visible above the ground level.

All the various ways we have of picturing religious life have some basis in reality. For there are various prisms through which we view all life, including religious life. Prisms are very important because they do provide a way for us to see, to highlight and to emphasize, to reject and to ignore. As others share their prisms of vision with us, we gain entrance to worlds of different colors and new life. Of course, if we maintain our vision only through our own prism, our world begins to take on a singleness of color and a frozen artificiality of life.

I do not want to wear out an image, but the kaleidoscope is another important way of looking. The prisms of a kaleidoscope produce their beauty through their relationships one to another. I find that the prisms through which we view life present us with adequate truth, new life, and fresh ways of acting only if we maintain the relationship of various viewpoints. That is the great strength of the church, who possesses various pictures of Jesus in her Gospels, who

Prisms for a Christ-Life

makes use of differing philosophies and theologies to foster understanding of her faith, and who approves the charisms of vastly differing forms of religious life to be legitimate icons of Christ for all the Christian faithful and for the world. It is in relationship that we maintain legitimacy, continuity, and true creativity.

Let Us Pray

Through Christ the universe was made, things seen and unseen.

Give thanks to the Father,
who made us fit
for the holy community of light
and rescued us from darkness,
bringing us into the realm
of his beloved Son
who redeemed us,
forgiving our sins.

Christ is an image
of the God we cannot see.
Christ is firstborn in all creation.

Before anything came to be, Christ was,
and the universe is held together by Christ.

COLOSSIANS 1:12-15, 17

The Charism of Religious Life

*R*eligious life in no way merits being called *dull*. Currently conferences, workshops, and books deal with the theme of "refounding religious life." Another approach looks more towards a "creating of religious life," often with the addition of "for the 21st century." We find ourselves confronted with various challenges which indicate that religious life remains a valuable concern not only for those who are dedicated to this special form of Christian living, but also for those who support it and are the collaborators and recipients of its service.

Religious life takes on its many different forms as responses to God's call to bridge anew the gap between the values of gospel and culture. Any particular grouping of religious challenges the rest of the church (including other religious) to a continuing conversion in one or other aspect of their Christian living. Religious frequently make uncomfortable the governing and teaching authority as well as their own benefactors and friends by their witness and service in those very areas where the church may be slipping into more secular values and ways of acting than gospel values and gospel acting. It is not surprising that religious have been in the forefront of the liberation-theology and base-community movement in Latin America.

The charism or grace which identifies the special call to a particular religious grouping often attracts some kind of participation by both diocesan priests and the laity. The "third orders" of some of the older religious institutes and the sodalities and secular branches of some other orders are examples of a long-standing tradition of affiliation. Today there are many more questions about various ways of *belonging* within the religious grouping—often referred to as "memberships" in the religious family. We are still in the early stages of this new focusing of collaboration in life and in ministry, and there are difficulties and obscurities still to be resolved. We will continue to find it necessary to clarify the identity and responsibilities of members dedicated in a specially graced form of life and of other parties with different vocations and yet somehow drawn by grace to a similar discipleship.

Religious life, with all its graced attempts to respond to gaps between the gospel and culture, today finds itself, along with the wider church and with the contemporary world, caught in the gap itself. As a result, the questions and issues will necessarily have only tentative responses while our church and world remain in this in-between time.

All of us continue to need prisms through which we may more quickly catch the movements and fleeting images of God's grace in our everyday religious life world. Each time we come to see a new aspect or see in new ways, we face the personal challenge of reintegrating the truth of our lives, our relationships, and our work.

Let Us Pray

Let morning announce your love, my God, for it is you I trust.

*Let morning announce your love,
for it is you I trust.
Show me the right way,
I offer you myself.*

*Rescue me from my foes,
you are my only refuge, Lord.*

Teach me your will,
for you are my God.

Graciously lead me, Lord,
on to level ground.
I call on your just name,
keep me safe, free from danger.

PSALM 143:8-11

Prisms for a Christ-Life

The Unifying Tradition
of Monasticism

*P*ope John Paul's apostolic letter *Orientale lumen* (The Light of the East) and the encyclical *Ut unum sint* (On Commitment to Ecumenism) offer us vision and direction. More than helps to enter these early years of the third millennium, they issue a call to conversion.

In *Orientale lumen* the pope emphasizes that our Eastern Catholic and our Orthodox brothers and sisters are earnest bearers of a venerable and ancient tradition integral to the church's heritage. He calls for all members of the church's Latin tradition to become fully acquainted with this treasure. He desires us all to be fired by a passionate longing that the church's catholicity become manifest to church members themselves and to the world, a catholicity comprising the several traditions together rather than in opposition to one another.

John Paul uses monasticism as a special vantage point from which to identify values important today for expressing the contribution of the Christian East to the journey of Christ's church towards the kingdom. In the East, monasticism, which did not experience the different kinds of apostolic life as in the West, is seen not merely as a separate category of Christians, but rather as a reference point for all the baptized, according to the gifts offered to each by the Lord. John Paul singles out the common traits uniting the monastic experience of the East and the West and forming a bridge of fellowship, "where unity as it is lived shines even more brightly than may appear in the dialogue between the churches." He emphasizes the splendid witness of nuns in the Christian East: "This witness has offered an example of giving full value in the church to what is specifically feminine, even breaking through the mentality of the time. During recent persecutions, especially in Eastern European countries, when many male monasteries were forcibly closed, female monasticism kept the torch of the monastic life burning. The nun's charism, with its own specific characteristics, is a visible sign of that motherhood of God to which Sacred Scripture often refers" (§9).

Among the values reflected in monasticism for the life of the church, the pope highlights (1) a balance in Christian life lived as a personal response to an individual call and as an ecclesial and community event; (2) a liturgy revealing the proper harmony of the baptized-in-Christ and the eucharistic meaning of all creation; (3) a maturing journey in terms of knowing self and being free and able to love as Jesus loves; (4) a tradition of spiritual guidance from brothers and sisters to whom the Spirit has granted this gift; (5) a community showing us a life of communion and service beginning in the family and extending to the wider community; (6) a unity of theology and spirituality deriving from the triune God—the principle and foundation of the Christian understanding that the human person is meant for and made for relationship; and (7) an all-pervading mystery, enveloped in awe, with which God presents us.

In still wider ways the encyclical *Ut unum sint* continues the call to deepen the unity we seek with one another and with God. Insisting that the unity of all Christians is God's will and is at the heart of the mission Christ entrusted to his followers, John Paul begs forgiveness for times when Catholics and the papacy itself have contributed to the divisions among Christians and calls for discussion about ways in which the pope can exercise power and authority in a reunited church. He notes that a heritage of saints belonging to all communities provides hope for the dialogue of conversion. "When we speak of a common heritage, we must acknowledge as part of it not only the institutions, rites, means of salvation, and the traditions which all the communities have preserved and by which they have been shaped, but first and foremost this reality of holiness" (§84).

The urgency of building for the future out of the strengths

of Christian heritages marks both of these papal writings. We, like the pope, need to set our sights on this unifying and evangelizing mission of all Christians.

Let Us Pray

**Blest are the pure of heart,
for they shall see God.**

*Lord, who is welcome in your house?
Who can rest on your holy mountain?*

*Those who walk with integrity
and do only what is right,
speaking the truth with courage.*

*They never spread slander
or abuse their friends
or condemn their neighbors.*

*They disdain the godless,
but honor those who believe.
Before God, they give their word
and keep it at any cost.*

*They neither lend for gain
nor take bribes against the guiltless.
These are the just:
they stand for ever unshaken.*

PSALM 15

Vita Consecrata and Transfiguration

*V*ita consecrata, the papal exhortation which completed the work of the synod of bishops dealing with consecrated life in the church, has been studied, but perhaps not nearly enough. Public reactions to the document among religious and church members at large seem to have been quite favorable.

Of course, there has been critique—inevitable, and absolutely necessary if there is to be continuing development and growth. One observation made immediately upon publication was about the daunting length of the document. Although there are only three chapters, along with an introduction and a conclusion, the text is substantial and typical of the dense style of writing associated with Pope John Paul. A saving factor in a long text is that there seems to be "something in it for everyone." Of course, there is likely something to disconcert everyone too.

Some have expressed dissatisfaction with the English translation "objective superiority" (§18 and §32) applied to consecrated life. Some are disappointed with the inconclusiveness of the equal stance of brothers in relation to priests in what is called a "mixed" institute; further work by a study commission is promised for a decision. While new forms of consecrated life are acknowledged and praised, a proposed commission to determine criteria of authenticity and of approval suggests a stance of caution. Although there is a strong positive stance towards the specific contribution of women religious, what is referred to as "new possibilities of presence and action on the part of consecrated women" may need more to be acknowledged as already a fact in many parts of the church than a future yet to be realized.

But, important as the resolution of these practical matters will continue to be for the proper development of consecrated lifeforms, I believe that the approach taken by the pope in the first chapter is hugely significant for a theological understanding and a spiritual appreciation of consecrated life. The pope does not take up the tools of philosophy, theology, anthropology, sociology, or behaviorial sciences for his primary approach to consecrated life. Instead he proposes the gospel passage of Jesus' transfiguration and suggests that we approach it as if it were an icon.

This transfiguration icon involves a gazing on the face of Jesus both in a "going up the mountain" and a "coming down the mountain." The pope refers to an ancient spiritual tradition which links the contemplative life to the prayer of Jesus on the mountain. But then he adds that the active dimension of consecrated life can be included because the transfiguration event serves as preparation to share with Jesus in the "toil of God's plan" and to be with him "courageously on the way of the cross."

In using the sacramentality of the icon, we Christians enter sacred time and space. Through a communion with the mystery signified by an icon, tradition holds that the believer is being made holy. An icon can be studied for the meanings of its symbolism, and so there is an intellectual component. Through reflections on various themes stimulated by the gospel passage, John Paul develops a contemporary understanding of consecrated life. But always the focus remains the icon giving us an *experience* of a divine world. For our understanding and appreciation of consecrated life, then, *Vita consecrata* presents us with a gospel text to suggest cognitive content and an iconic vision of the divine: by gazing upon the face of Jesus, we enter into the mystery of consecrated life in the church and its centering world of holiness.

Let Us Pray

Show us the radiance of your mercy, God.

Show us mercy, God of all,
teach every land to fear you.
Strike boldly against the enemy,
display your power.

Make them an example of your glory,
as we once showed them your holiness.
Then they will know what we know:
there is no God but you.
Forge new signs, new wonders
with your strong right hand.

Gather every tribe of Jacob
to reclaim its birthright.
Be kind to Israel, your firstborn,
to the people who bear your name.

Deal gently with Jerusalem,
your holy city,
where your throne is fixed.
Fill Zion with your splendor,
your temple with your glory.

Make real the vision
prophets spoke in your name;
keep faith with what you began.
Reward those who hope in you,
prove the prophets right.

Answer the pleas of the faithful
and favor us as always.
Then the world will know
that you are God for ever.

SIRACH 36:1-7, 13, 16-22

Prisms for a Christ-Life

Boundaries and Life

*B*oundaries are a part of life. We think of how boundaries identify our countries and our states, our soccer fields and our tennis courts. Behavior to be proper and humor to be appreciated observe boundaries. There are time boundaries for speeches to be effective and financial limits for buying and selling.

Sometimes we see boundaries through a negative filter. We talk about how we do not want to feel bound in any way since that would close off possible opportunities for ourselves. Boundaries, we say, are restrictions on our human potential and freedom. Yet as a counterpoint we also experience that, when cancer breaks down boundaries and has metastasized, life becomes diminished and threatened. So too, when people do not acknowledge certain boundaries to their own stamina, they can have a breakdown or become sick. Although sometimes appearing to us to be restrictive, boundaries, then, can be appreciated in a life system for the part they play in maintaining good health and vibrant life. Witness the negative results when we humans do not observe boundaries in our polluting of streams and oceans, in our poisoning the atmosphere through chemical emissions, and in our destroying world weather patterns through the deforesting in the Amazon basin.

Sometimes people, including women and men religious, see religious life as mostly boundaries that confine rather than a frame that enhances. Whether it be the observance of the traditional evangelical counsels of chastity, poverty, and obedience, the acceptance of a life in common, or the practice of enclosure, religious life has always had boundaries. But through an ecological perspective—that is, religious life identified as a life system—we can come to a fresh appreciation of the vital quality that boundaries contribute.

Today, when for many religious congregations *inclusiveness* seems to eliminate all boundaries, we could ask ourselves whether in a life-system model this movement is going towards health. When there are no boundaries to the kinds of ministries taken on by members of a congregation and no boundaries to what constitutes a life together, we might wonder whether a deadly cancer may likely enough be coursing through a life system. Since we are so conscious today of environmental and ecological concerns with a scientific realism never before possible, we need to apply a similar kind of care to religious life identified as an ecological system. Then our acceptance of certain boundaries will be situated within the context of health and vitality.

Evangelical counsels, community life, and the enclosure associated with contemplative life are all boundaries—boundaries connected with a furtherance of life. Aging, too, is a boundary—difficult to face for active, service-oriented people—but aging is seen by faith as another stage in our growing in Christ. Yet doubts, even so, assail us: How can the restrictions of aging, a kind of final boundary of human life, be seen as a growing?

The church observance of the Lenten and Easter seasons invites us always to contemplate the growth potential of all the boundaries of human life portrayed in Jesus' paschal mystery. Jesus makes even death no longer a limitation but a boundary that issues into life. We see that Jesus does not take away the boundary of death, but rather allows it—in daily actions and in our final human act—to become the key to our entering into his own paschal mystery, culminating in new and surprising life. Our desire to identify with this paschal mystery as a way of daily living leads us to view all boundaries through the perspective of the risen Jesus. Boundaries, it seems, bring home to us how much we find life as Easter people.

Prisms for a Christ-Life

Let Us Pray

**At the name of Jesus every knee will bend
in heaven and on earth.**

*Though in the form of God,
Jesus did not claim
equality with God
but emptied himself,
taking the form of a slave,
human like one of us.*

*Flesh and blood,
he humbled himself,
obeying to the death,
death on a cross.
For this very reason
God lifted him high
and gave him the name
above all names.*

*So at the name of Jesus
every knee will bend
in heaven, on earth,
and in the world below,
and every tongue exclaim
to the glory of God the Father,
"Jesus Christ is Lord."*

PHILIPPIANS 2:6-11

Psalm and Scripture
References